Mountain Biking
the Appalachians

Brevard-Asheville/
The Pisgah Forest

MOUNTAIN BIKING THE APPALACHIANS

Brevard-Asheville/The Pisgah Forest

by
Lori Finley

John F. Blair, Publisher
Winston-Salem, North Carolina

BOOK DESIGN BY DEBRA LONG HAMPTON

MAPS BY THE ROBERTS GROUP

PRINTED AND BOUND BY R. R. DONNELLEY & SONS

COVER PHOTOGRAPH—

Crossing Fletcher Creek in the North Mills River Area

Library of Congress Cataloging-In-Publication Data

Finley, Lori, 1958–
     Mountain biking the Appalachians. Brevard-Asheville/the Pisgah Forest /
Lori Finley.
          p.   cm.
     Includes index.
     ISBN 0-89587-136-X
     1. Bicycle touring—North Carolina—Pisgah National Forest—Guidebooks.
     2. All terrain cycling—North Carolina—Pisgah National Forest—Guidebooks.
     3. Pisgah National Forest (N.C.)—Guidebooks.   I. Title.
     GV1045.5.N752P574   1995
     796.6'4'0975694—dc20   95-30396

For Suzanne

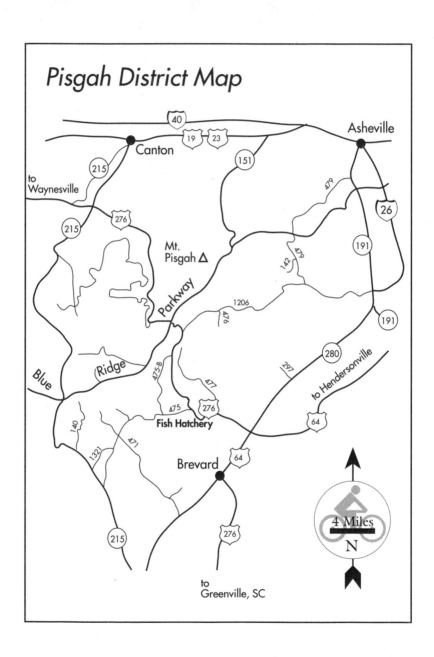

Contents

North Mills River Area

Pink Beds/South Mills River Area

Acknowledgments

My heartfelt thanks go to all of my friends who pedaled along as I researched the trails for this book. I could not have done it without them. I reserve special thanks for my two comrades, Herb Clark and Joel McCollough, who explored the majority of these routes with me. They rarely complained, even when they had to stop and wait while I made notes, or when we took wrong turns, or when trails petered out into tangles of dense underbrush, or when temperatures were extreme, or when I crashed and had to be plucked out of the twisted wreckage that was once my bike, or when we drove home late at night, cold and hungry. Others who cycled with me and deserve a word of thanks are Midge Luttrell, Jeff Tollison, Steve White, Megan the Wonder Dog, Miller Putnam, Sandra Thomas, Fred Thomas, Lewis Lyda, Mark Holden, Karen Burgoyne, and Jason Howell.

I am especially indebted to Ed Erwin for his helpful editing and his route suggestions.

Thanks go to the United States Forest Service staff of the Pisgah District—particularly Sue Elderkin—for their help and their progressive attitude toward mountain biking.

Thanks go to Wes Gattis of Sunrift Adventures, who gave me the idea for this book.

Thanks go to Skip Snow and Boney at Sunshine Cycle Shop for keeping my wheels spinning.

Thanks go to Linda and Tom Kovach for their love, their support, and their help in finding the right publisher.

Thanks go to my wonderful parents, who convinced me at an early age that I could do anything.

Thanks go to my sweet daughters, Erin and Elizabeth, for their patience with and pride in their unconventional mom.

And most important, thanks go to my husband, Bob, who inspired me, sustained me, and cheered me on as I crossed the finish line.

Introduction

The high mountains and deep valleys of Pisgah National Forest are a veritable mecca for mountain-biking enthusiasts. There are over 200 miles of designated mountain-bike trails which draw droves of cyclists of diverse abilities to the area each year. These trails meander into and out of hardwood coves, snake along the lush banks of mountain streams, and challenge riders by ascending to overlooks close to 5,000 feet high, thereby offering spectacular views of the surrounding Blue Ridge Mountains. By combining these trails with the multitude of logging roads, forest-service roads, and dirt roads in the area, riders can enjoy a labyrinth of mountain-bike routes.

Hundreds of years ago, this area teemed with game and rich vegetation. It was home to the Cherokee Indians, who called it "Warwasseeta." The area was not dubbed "Pisgah" until the late 1700s. The name comes from the fourth chapter of Deuteronomy; Moses stood on the mountain called Pisgah when he first gazed upon the Promised Land of the people of Israel. In 1776, an expedition led by General Griffith Rutherford came to the mountains to drive out the Cherokee. Among the group was a soldier and preacher named James Hall. When he first stood in the French Broad River Valley and looked up at the mountainous area now known as Pisgah, Hall gazed upon a land of milk and honey, a promised land. It is Reverend Hall who is credited with recalling the name from the Bible and applying it to the mountain region looming before him.

In the late 1800s, George Vanderbilt also viewed this area south of Asheville as a promised land. By 1888, he had acquired an estimated 125,000 acres of it. Vanderbilt built the famous Biltmore House in Asheville, which is open to the public for tours. In 1911, new legislation permitted the United States Forest Service to purchase forest lands for the first time. Nearly 80,000 acres—including Mount Pisgah—were purchased from the Vanderbilt family to help form the 479,000-acre tract known today as Pisgah National Forest.

The Pisgah District is the most popular of the four districts of Pisgah National Forest. It draws millions of visitors annually. It is an exceptionally beautiful land of cascading waterfalls, steep, rocky balds, frothy whitewater rivers spilling over glistening rocks, sun-dappled meadows, towering hemlock trees with lacy evergreen boughs, and panoramic vistas of surrounding mountains and verdant valleys.

Many of the trails in the forest are well-suited for mountain bikes and have been designated for such use; mountain bikes are not allowed in designated wilderness or on the Blue Ridge Parkway trails, however. The rides described in this book are some of the most popular in the Pisgah District. They are given a subjective difficulty rating based on length, elevation change, and trail condition. Many of these routes have special features which make them especially memorable. However, don't discount a ride simply because it doesn't lead past a waterfall or an outstanding overlook; each of these rides has a beauty and worth of its own.

Planning a Trip

Location
Pisgah National Forest is located in western North Carolina near Brevard and Asheville.

Routes
The routes described in this book are grouped into regions based on the origin of the ride. Any ride can be completed in a day, many of them in half a day.

Before You Go
Before riding, it is advisable to check with the Pisgah District Ranger Station (704-877-3265) to confirm that the ride is open for mountain-bike use. At the time of this writing, all the routes covered were open to mountain bikers. But as we all know, a cloud of land-use controversy hangs over many mountain-biking areas. Land status is in a constant state of flux, and designations do change. **You** are ultimately responsible for ensuring that a trail is legal for pedaling. If you arrive at a trailhead and find that a No Mountain Biking sign has been posted, heed it. There are always plenty of other rides nearby.

Maps
This guide, or any guide, should be used in conjunction with forest service maps or quad maps. Each ride description includes a list of maps that feature the trail or ride.

Seasons
Because of the relatively mild winters in western North Carolina, trails can be ridden year-round. Occasionally, they will be

covered by snow or ice. Some trails require river or creek crossings and should be avoided during cold weather due to the risk of hypothermia. There are also some trails that should be avoided after periods of heavy rain because of muddy conditions. These special considerations are noted in the individual ride descriptions. Mountain showers can be expected almost every day during the summer and are often a welcome, cooling relief from the heat. Hunting is permitted in the forest during the autumn months; mountain bikers are advised to wear fluorescent orange or some other bright, unnatural color.

Equipment and Essentials

Bicycle

A mountain bike with fat, knobby tires is necessary for most of these rides. Some trails are not technically challenging and can be ridden with either a full-fledged mountain bike or an all-terrain bicycle; this is noted in the individual ride descriptions.

Cyclocomputer

A cyclocomputer will make the directions in this book easier to follow as turns and special features are noted in increments to a tenth of a mile. Where possible, special features or landmarks at trail turnoffs have been noted for the benefit of cyclists without computers. You can complete these trips without one, but the chance of getting lost or missing a side trail to a waterfall or other highlight is increased. Variations in tire pressures, tire sizes, individual cyclist's weight, and in individual cyclocomputers can produce different mileage readings over identical paths. Your readings may not always agree with those provided in this book, but they should be close.

Tool Kit

Many of these trails wind through secluded, remote areas of the forest, so a tool kit is highly recommended.

The most common mechanical problem on the trail is a flat tire. Be certain you have a bicycle pump, tire irons, and a patch kit or a spare tube with you. If you have never changed a flat tire, learn how and practice at home before your ride. And if you are mechanically inept (like me), bring along a friend who knows what a chain rivet tool and an Allen wrench are and, better yet, knows how to use them. I have seen some impressive repairs out on the trail that have kept riders riding. Even a broken derailleur doesn't necessarily mean hoofing it back to the car; the right tool and a little ingenuity can have you up and spinning again, even though you will be limited to a single gear.

First-aid Kit

Again, many of these trails are in remote sections of forest where the rescue index is poor. Bring a small, well-appointed first-aid kit with you. It is also a good idea to include a stubby candle and matches in the kit. In winter, you would not want to leave an injured rider without a warming fire while you sought medical assistance.

Water

When it comes to water, I have two pieces of advice: Bring your own, and bring enough. The creeks and rivers may look pristine, but gone are the days when cyclists could dip their water bottles into a cold mountain stream for an easy refill. There are some bad bugs around, the most notable being giardia. This single-celled organism can wreak havoc in your intestines if allowed to set up residence. So how much should you bring? You know your needs better than anyone else, but take a minimum of two water bottles. For long, strenuous rides or hot-weather rides, you'll need more. Sure, extra water adds weight, but staying well hydrated is of critical importance.

Safety

The United States Forest Service makes the following recommendations for safety in the back country:

1. Always let someone know where you are going, what route you are taking, when you expect to return, and what to do if you don't.
2. Check the weather forecast. Be prepared with proper clothing and equipment for all potential weather conditions.
3. Don't push yourself beyond your limits.
4. Keep an eye on each other.
5. Plot your progress on a map as you travel. Know where you are at all times.

Etiquette

Mountain bikers are the new kids on the block, or rather the new kids in the woods. We must be cognizant of the rights of others in the forest and treat others with courtesy. It takes only a few discourteous, irresponsible acts of destructive trail riding to close a trail to mountain bikes permanently. Ride responsibly. The National Off Road Bicycle Association (NORBA) promotes the following guidelines:

1. Yield the right of way to other nonmotorized recreationists. Realize that people judge all cyclists by your actions.
2. Slow down and use caution when approaching or overtaking another, and make your presence known well in advance.
3. Maintain control of your speed at all times, and approach turns in anticipation of someone around the bend.
4. Stay on designated trails to avoid trampling native vegetation, and minimize potential erosion to trails by not using muddy trails or short-cutting switchbacks.
5. Do not disturb wildlife or livestock.
6. Do not litter. Pack out what you pack in, and pack out more than your share whenever possible.
7. Respect public and private property, including trail-use signs and No Trespassing signs; leave gates as you found them.
8. Be self-sufficient, and let your destination and speed be determined by your ability, your equipment, the terrain, and present and potential weather conditions.
9. Do not travel solo when "bikepacking" in remote areas. Leave word of your destination and when you plan to return.
10. Observe the practice of minimum-impact bicycling by "taking only pictures and memories and leaving only waffle prints."
11. Always wear a helmet whenever you ride.

Many of the trails in Pisgah National Forest are also used by equestrians, so exercise courtesy when you encounter horses. Always dismount and give the horse the right of way. If you approach the horse from the front, dismount and stand on the side of the trail. Stay in the horse's line of vision; wait to remount until it has moved well away. If you approach a horse from the rear, dismount and walk slowly until the rider notices you. The rider should move off the trail to allow you to walk your bike past. Remount when you are well away from the horse. If the rider doesn't move off the trail, ask him how he would like you to pass so that you won't spook his horse.

Accommodations

Campgrounds

Primitive camping is permitted district-wide 1,000 feet from an open road. Roadside camping is permitted only in sites designated by an Overnight Camping Allowed sign. Vehicles must remain parked on the road shoulder; pull-offs have been provided on many forest roads for this purpose. The following campgrounds are managed by the Pisgah District:

1. Davidson River Campground (161 campsites, showers)
2. Sunburst Recreation Area (10 campsites)
3. North Mills River Campground (28 campsites, open year-round)
4. Lake Powhatan Campground (98 campsites, showers)

For seasonal dates, call the ranger station at 704-877-3265. The ranger station can also give you information on group campgrounds for large groups.

Mount Pisgah Campground, located on the Blue Ridge Parkway, is privately managed. It is a primitive campground with no electricity or showers. For information, call the Pisgah Inn at 704-235-8228.

Motels

There are many motels and inns in nearby Brevard and Asheville. For current lodging information, call the Brevard Chamber of Commerce at 704-883-3700 or the Asheville Chamber of Commerce at 704-258-3858.

Davidson River Area

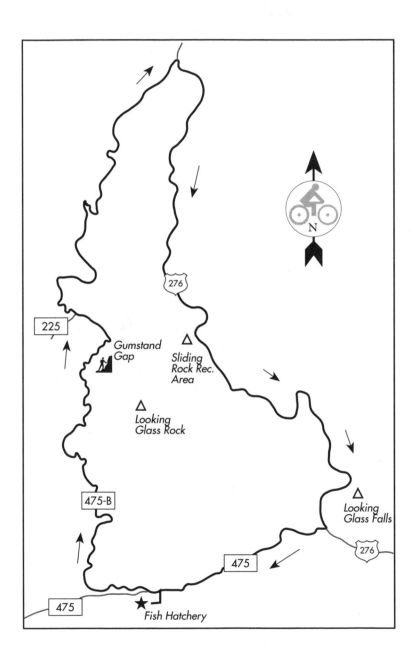

225

276

Gumstand
Gap

Sliding
Rock Rec.
Area

Looking
Glass Rock

475-B

Looking
Glass Falls

276

475

475

★ Fish Hatchery

N

Headwaters Road / U.S. 276 / Sliding Rock / Looking Glass Falls Loop

Distance: 13. 2 miles

Difficulty: Moderate

Riding Surface: Gravel road, paved road

Maps: 1. USGS 7.5 minute quadrangle, Shining Rock
2. Pisgah District Trail Map

Access: From the ranger station, proceed north on U.S. 276 for 3.5 miles to the junction with F.R. 475 (Davidson River Road). Proceed 1.5 miles to the Pisgah Forest Fish Hatchery parking lot.

Elevation change: You will begin at 2,400 feet and climb to a maximum elevation of 3, 200 feet just past Gumstand Gap. You will maintain this elevation as you cycle F.R. 475B (Headwaters Road) through Case Ridge Gap toward U.S. 276. You will then gently descend to 2,800 feet at Sliding Rock and on to a minimum of 2,400 feet at Looking Glass Falls. The total elevation gain is 800 feet.

Season: This loop of roads is open year-round to mountain bikes. However, it should be avoided on busy weekends and holidays due to heavy automobile traffic on U.S. 276.

If you are not a single-track purist, you will love this moderate loop of dirt roads and paved roads. This ride carves a path through exceptionally beautiful mountains and stops off at some of the most popular attractions in Pisgah National Forest, such as Sliding Rock and Looking Glass Falls. Sliding Rock will appeal to any young or young-at-heart cyclists riding in your group. Thousands of gallons of water spill over smooth granite each minute to form a glistening, 60-foot natural water slide which draws droves of thrill seekers and spectators in the summer months. A few miles past Sliding Rock, you will see a long parking area on the left; it is generally filled with the cars of tourists who flock to view and photograph Looking Glass Falls during the forest's busy season. It is here that the Davidson River squeezes down to a width of 30 feet and then hurls itself over a rocky cliff to drop 60 vertical feet in an unbroken rush of white water into a pool below. Looking Glass Falls is considered one of the most beautiful waterfalls in western North Carolina and should not be missed.

The ride begins on F.R. 475B, a scenic dirt road which parallels Rockhouse Creek for a few miles and climbs toward the bald face of Looking Glass Rock. This is another popular attraction in Pisgah National Forest and is frequently dotted with intrepid rock climbers during warm weather. After about 3 miles of fairly intense climbing, you will reach Gumstand Gap, which offers a spectacular view of the "nose" of Looking Glass Rock and a good resting spot to catch your breath. The ride continues on F.R. 475B and maintains an elevation of 3,200 feet while passing through Case Ridge Gap, which skirts the base of Case Camp Ridge.

After turning right onto U.S. 276, you will pass Sliding Rock and Looking Glass Falls as you make a fast, fun descent back to the fish hatchery. Visitors are welcome at the hatchery, which raises 60,000 trout annuallly to stock the streams of Pisgah National Forest. The "raceways," or tanks, at the hatchery contain many different species of trout, such as brook, brown, and rainbow.

The brook trout, or speckled trout, is the only species native to the eastern United States and is the least timid of the different trout species. It is a gluttonous fish that will bite at almost any kind of lure, yet it has fastidious requirements for clean, cold water. The number of brook trout found in southeastern mountain streams has dwindled considerably in past years due to competition with rainbow trout. Today, they are generally found only in extremely remote high-elevation rivers, where conditions are more pristine. By contrast, the brown trout, which hails from Europe, is the wariest of species. Its cautious nature and its ability to thrive in warmer, less clean water make it a better survivor in the Southeast than the brook trout. The rainbow trout, which is native to the western United States, has characteristics which fall somewhere between those of brook and brown trout.

As you walk beside the tanks, it is interesting to note the different responses the species have to humans hovering above them. Their contrasting degrees of wariness are evident as the brook trout race toward the onlookers, congregate en masse, and excitedly jump into the air, while the brown trout appear frightened and immediately swim as far away from onlookers as possible.

Sliding Rock

0.0 From the fish hatchery parking lot, cross the bridge over the Davidson River and ride to the stop sign. Turn left.

0.2 You will immediately come to a fork; take the right fork, which is F.R. 475B. This dirt road begins a mild ascent which quickly increases to a substantial gradient. Rockhouse Creek parallels the road on the left and is flanked by hemlock, laurel, and rhododendron. F.R. 475B is open to traffic, so watch for vehicles.

1.5 Slickrock Trail, which leads to the south face of Looking Glass Rock, is on the right. (No bikes are allowed on this trail.)

3.2 The Sunwall trailhead can be seen to the right; this is a trail used predominantly by rock climbers heading to Looking Glass Rock and is off-limits to mountain bikes. Just beyond this trail are a gravel parking area and a grassy resting spot at Gumstand Gap. At this point, the road begins a moderate descent.

3.5 The road intersects with F.R. 225; continue by bearing to the right.

6.4 F.R. 475B intersects with U.S. 276; turn right and begin a gentle descent.

8.8 The Sliding Rock recreation area is on the right.

10.8 Looking Glass Falls is on the left.

11.4 U.S. 276 intersects with F.R. 475; turn right to return to the fish hatchery parking lot.

13.2 You will arrive back at the parking lot.

Looking Glass Falls

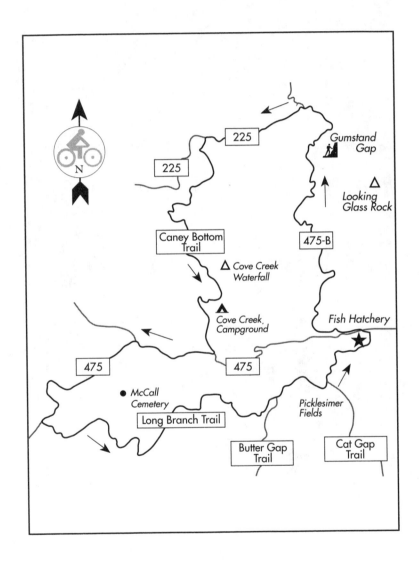

Headwaters Road /
West-side Caney Bottom Trail /
Long Branch Trail /
Butter Gap Trail Loop

Distance: 14.4 miles

Difficulty: Moderate

Riding surface: Gravel road, single-track

Maps: 1. USGS 7.5 minute quadrangle, Shining Rock
2. Pisgah District Trail Map

Access: From the ranger station, proceed north on U.S. 276 for 3.5 miles to the junction with F.R. 475 (Davidson River Road). Proceed 1.5 miles to the Pisgah Forest Fish Hatchery parking lot.

Elevation change: You will begin at 2,400 feet and climb to 3,200 feet by the time you reach the fork in F.R. 475B (Headwaters Road) at 3.5 miles. This is the highest point in the ride. You will then descend to 2,600 feet at Cove Creek Group Campground before beginning another climb on F.R. 475 up to 3,100 feet at the Long Branch trailhead. Then comes a descent back to 2,400 feet. The total elevation gain is 1,300 feet.

Season: All roads and trails comprising this loop are open to mountain bikes year-round, witht he exception of the section of Butter Gap Trail, which is open only from October 15 through April 15. Therefore, this loop must be avoided during the summer months. A year-round loop which does not include Butter Gap Trail is described in the next chapter.

With its rolling terrain, inviting meadows, exhilarating creek crossings, and eye-catching vistas of ascending forest, this loop of single-track trails and dirt roads affords mountain bikers of diverse abilities an enjoyable day of riding. The loop begins on F.R. 475B, a picturesque road which winds its way up toward the regal stone face of Looking Glass Rock. The road follows a moderately steep grade which gives riders a good warmup for the day ahead. There is a fork in the road not far from Gumstand Gap; cyclists should bear left onto F.R. 225 to continue this loop.

At about 4.5 miles, Caney Bottom Extension Trail is on the left. The trail plunges bumpily through the woods and across stony creeks. After a couple of miles, the loop continues on an ascending dirt road until Long Branch Trail is seen on the left. This trail, narrow at the beginning, weaves through grassy glades and rhododendron that is especially resplendent in the early summer, when it is dressed in pink and white blossoms. McCall Cemetery rests 250 yards off the trail and is a somber reminder of the colony of settlers who lived here back in the 1800s. Toward the end of the loop, Long Branch Trail becomes more challenging, climbing briefly along an eroded, steep section. An easy, fun ride through Picklesimer Fields and then to Grogan Creek marks the end of the ride.

Long Branch Trail

0.0 From the fish hatchery parking lot, cross the bridge over the Davidson River to the stop sign. Turn left.

0.2 You will immediately come to a fork; take the right fork, which is F.R. 475B. This dirt road begins a mild ascent that quickly increases to a substantial gradient. The beautiful scenery of hemlock, laurel, rhododendron, and small streams will help you forget the climbing dirt road looming ahead. F.R. 475B is open to traffic, so watch for vehicles.

1.5 Slickrock Trail, which leads to the south face of Looking Glass Rock, is on the right. (No bikes are allowed on this trail.)

3.3 The trail off to the right is called Sunwall. It is used predominantly by rock climbers heading to Looking Glass rock and is off-limits to mountain bikes. Just beyond this trail are a gravel parking area and a grassy resting spot at Gumstand Gap. At this point, the road begins a moderate descent.

3.6 There is a fork in the road; take the left road, F.R. 225. There is a moderate climb which is followed by a long, steep descent to Caney Bottom Extension Trail.

4.5 Turn left at Caney Bottom Extension, a grassy, old gated logging road. After turning, you will come almost immediately to a fork. Turn right and follow the yellow blaze. Pedal straight down the trail and cross the logging road.

4.9 You will come to a creek crossing. A footbridge is located here for those who do not wish to ride across the creek.

5.0 You will reach an intersection of trails. Markers indicate that the Caney Bottom Trail (east leg) is to the right, Caney Bottom Extension Trail is to the left. Do not turn; continue straight.

5.7 Bear left and continue downhill; you will cross Caney Bottom Creek. There is a sturdy footbridge with a railing.

6.7 A narrow hiking trail to Cove Creek Waterfall is on the left. Continue straight after dismounting and viewing the waterfall.

7.2 The trail makes a 90-degree left turn toward Cove Creek Group Campground. Almost immediately after the sharp turn in the trail, turn right and continue on this blue-blazed trail. (The campground is for campers only; mountain bikers are required to pedal around the sites.)

7.4 After crossing a small creek, you will reach a T-intersection; turn left.

7.5 Turn right onto the gravel road.

7.7 You will come to a deep crossing of Caney Bottom Creek. For a dry crossing, use the wooden bridge on the left.

7.8 Pedal around gate, then turn right onto F.R. 475, Davidson River Road.

10.0 Cemetery Loop Trail (foot travel only) is on the left.

10.1 The Long Branch trailhead is on the left. A sign shows the distances to McCall Cemetery (0.8 mile), Butter Gap Trail (2.7 miles), and the fish hatchery (4.1 miles).

10.9 There is an intersection of trails. Long branch Trail turns to the right. Straight ahead is a trail leading 250 yards to McCall Cemetery.

12.0 The trail turns sharply to the left and plunges into a grassy meadow. The trail across the meadow is heavily bordered by thorny blackberry bushes.

12.7 The trail veers to the right. There is a log blazed with orange to direct cyclists and hikers. Exercise caution on this steep, technical descent.

12.8 Long Branch Trail ends at the intersection of trails. Butter Gap Trail turns to the right and to the left. Turn left onto Butter Gap Trail.

13.0 The trail spills into a grassy, open area known as Picklesimer Fields. This is an easy, fun blast toward the end of the ride.

13.4 Several trails bleed into the intersection with Cat Gap Trail. There is a large boulder in the center of the trail; bear right and you can cycle around it. Turn left onto Cat Gap Trail. The trail is level and in great condition. Grogan Creek is on the right.

13.7 There is a fork in the trail. Bear left onto the un-marked trail toward the forest-service road. The right (lower) fork is for hikers.

14.0 Turn left onto the forest-service road. (To the right is Robert's Bridge over Grogan Creek. The bridge leads to a trail back to the fish hatchery; this trail is for foot travel only.)

14.1 Enter the parking lot behind the fish hatchery. Cycle around the buildings and the fish pools.

14.4 You will arrive back at the main fish hatchery parking lot.

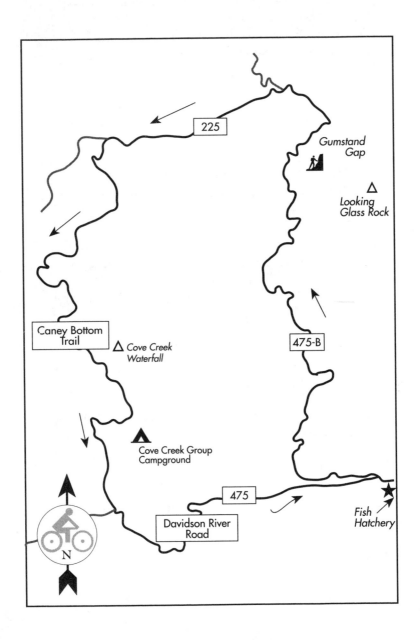

225

Gumstand
Gap

△
Looking
Glass Rock

Caney Bottom
Trail

△ Cove Creek
Waterfall

475-B

Cove Creek Group
Campground

475

Davidson River
Road

Fish
Hatchery

N

Headwaters Road / West-side Caney Bottom Trail Loop

Distance: 9.8 miles

Difficulty: Moderate

Riding surface: Gravel road, single-track

Maps: 1. USGS 7.5 minute quadrangle, Shining Rock
2. Pisgah District Trail Map

Access: From the ranger station, proceed north on U.S. 276 for 3.5 miles to the junciton with F.R. 475 (Davidson River Road). Proceed 1.5 miles to the Pisgah Forest Fish Hatchery parking lot.

Elevation change: You will begin at 2,400 feet and climb to 3,200 feet by the time you reach the fork in F.R. 475B (Headwaters Road) at 3.5 miles. This is the highest point in the ride. You will descend to 2,600 feet at Cove Creek Group Campground and then gently descend 200 feet more back to the fish hatchery parking lot. The total elevation gain is 800 feet.

Season: This loop configuration is open year-round to mountain bikes.

Meadow on Caney Bottom Trail

This is a combination of dirt road and single-track trail where a mountain bike fits perfectly. Gently rolling terrain, inviting meadows, exhilarating creek crossings, and eye-catching vistas of ascending forest assure you of a fine day of riding.

This moderate loop begins at the fish hatchery. Take a left at the stop sign and then a right at the fork in the road. F.R. 475B, a picturesque dirt road, winds its way up toward the regal stone face of Looking Glass Rock, which is often decorated with rock climbers during warm weather. Flanked by hemlock, mountain laurel, and an occasional trout stream, the road follows a moderately steep grade which gives riders a good warmup for the day ahead. There is a fork in the road not far from Gumstand Gap; cyclists should bear left onto F.R. 225 to continue this loop.

At about 4.5 miles, you will see the Caney Bottom Extension trailhead on the left. The trail plunges bumpily across stony creeks and spills onto F.R. 475 after a couple of miles. Turn left to begin a gentle descent down this dirt road back to the fish hatchery parking lot.

0.0 From the fish hatchery parking lot, cross the bridge over the Davidson River to the stop sign. Turn left.

0.2 You will immediately come to a fork; take the right fork, which is F.R. 475B. This dirt road begins a mild ascent that quickly increases to a substantial gradient. The beautiful scenery of hemlock, laurel, rhododen-dron, and small streams will help you forget the climbing dirt road looming ahead. F.R. 475B is open to traffic, so watch for vehicles.

1.5 Slickrock Trail, which leads to the south face of Looking Glass Rock, is on the right. (No bikes are allowed on this trail.)

3.3 The trail off to the right, called Sunwall, is closed to mountain bikes. It is used predominantly by rock climbers heading to Looking Glass Rock. Just beyond this trail are a gravel parking area and a grassy resting

Caney Bottom Trail

spot at Gumstand Gap. At this point, the road begins a moderate descent.

3.6 There is a fork in the road; take the left road, F.R. 225. There is a moderate climb which is followed by a long, steep descent to Caney Bottom Extension Trail.

4.5 Turn left at Caney Bottom Extension, a grassy, old gated logging road. You will come almost immediately to a fork. Turn right and follow the yellow blaze. Pedal straight down the trail and cross the logging road.

4.9 You will come to a creek crossing. A footbridge is located here for those who do not wish to ride across the creek.

5.0 You will reach an intersection of trails. Markers indicate that the Caney Bottom Trail (east leg) is to the right, Caney Bottom Extension Trail is to the left. Do not turn; continue straight.

Creek crossing

5.7 Bear left and continue downhill; you will cross Caney Bottom Creek. A sturdy footbridge with a hand railing spans the creek.

6.7 A narrow hiking trail to Cove Creek Waterfalls is to the left. Continue straight after dismounting and viewing the falls.

7.2 The trail makes a 90-degree left turn toward Cove Creek Group Campground. Almost immediately after the sharp turn in the trail, turn right and continue on this blue-blazed trail. (The campground is for campers only; mountain bikers are required to pedal around the sites.)

7.4 After crossing a small creek, you will reach a T-intersection; turn left.

7.5 Turn right onto the gravel road.

7.7 You will come to a deep crossing of Caney Bottom Creek. For a dry crossing, use the wooden bridge on the left.

7.8 Pedal around gate, then turn left onto F.R. 475, Davidson River Road.

9.8 You will arrive back at the parking lot.

Note: If time permits, you may find a walk through the fish hatchery interesting. The pools, or "raceways," contain many different species and sizes of trout. The hatchery raises 60,000 trout each year to stock the streams of Pisgah National Forest.

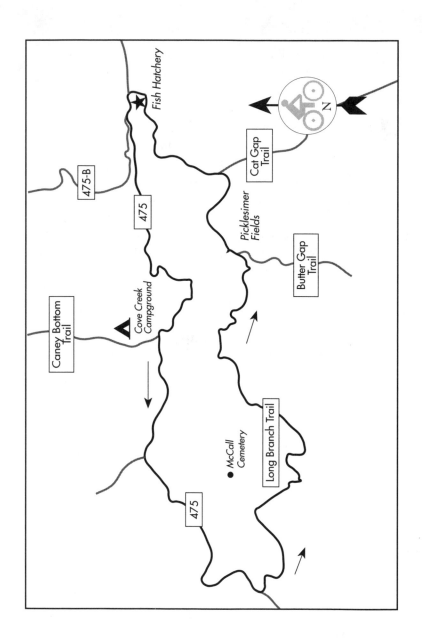

Fish Hatchery

475-B

475

Caney Bottom
Trail

Cove Creek
Campground

Cat Gap
Trail

Picklesimer
Fields

Butter Gap
Trail

N

McCall
Cemetery

Long Branch Trail

475

Long Branch Trail Loop

Distance: 8.5 miles

Difficulty: Moderate

Riding surface: Gravel road, single-track

Maps: 1. USGS 7.5 minute quadrangle, Shining Rock
2. Pisgah District Trail Map

Access: From the ranger station, proceed north on U.S. 276 for 3.5 miles to the junction with F.R. 475 (Davidson River Road). Proceed 1.5 miles to the Pisgah Forest Fish Hatchery parking lot.

Elevation change: You will begin at 2,400 feet and climb to 2,600 feet by the time you reach the trail to Cove Creek Group Campground at about 2 miles. You will reach the highest point, 3,100 feet, at the Long Branch trailhead. After turning onto this trail, you will begin your descent to the fish hatchery. The total elevation gain is 700 feet.

Season: Long Branch Trail is open year-round to mountain bikes, but the short section of Butter Gap Trail that runs through Picklesimer Fields is open to mountain bikes only from October 15 through April 15. Therefore, this loop should be ridden only during the winter.

This loop configuration is a scenic combination of climbing dirt road and descending single-track trail. The Davidson River, a beautifully pristine trout stream, parallels the road for a few miles and makes the steady ascent almost enjoyable. The initial section of Long Branch Trail is a narrow, old log pull, and its plunging descent is a welcome respite from the grinding climb of F.R. 475. The trail is mostly level but is spiced with a few climbs and technical descents and several creek crossings. Cyclists will pedal through a mélange of sunny meadows, thickets of mountain laurel, and heavily canopied, dark hemlock forests. McCall Cemetery, a scattering of simple tombstones on top of the ridge, is the final resting place of a colony of settlers who lived here in the 1800s.

0.0   After parking at the fish hatchery, cycle back over the bridge and turn left at the stop sign.

0.2   You will immediately come to a fork in the road; take the left fork, which is F.R. 475. The Davidson River, to the left, parallels the road for several miles.

Long Branch Trail

1.9 A trail off to the right leads to Cove Creek Group Campground. (In case you need to refill your water bottles, there is a water pump at the campground. If a group is camped there, ask permission from the group leader first.) Continue straight on F.R. 475 to the Long Branch trailhead.

4.1 Cemetery Loop Trail (foot travel only) is on the left.

4.2 The Long Branch trailhead is on the left. A sign shows the distances to McCall Cemetery (0.8 mile), Butter Gap Trail (2.7 miles), and the fish hatchery (4.1 miles).

5.0 There is an intersection of trails. Long Branch Trail turns to the right. Straight ahead is a trail leading 250 yards to McCall Cemetery.

6.1 The trail turns sharply to the left and plunges into a grassy meadow. It continues across the meadow and is heavily bordered by thorny blackberry bushes.

6.8 The trail veers to the right. There is a log blazed with orange to direct cyclists and hikers. Exercise caution on this steep, technical descent.

6.9 Long Branch Trail ends at the intersection of trails. Butter Gap Trail goes to the right and to the left. Turn left onto Butter Gap Trail.

7.1 The trail spills into a grassy, open area known as Picklesimer Fields. This is an easy, fun blast toward the end of the ride.

7.5 There is another intersection of trails. There is a large boulder blocking the trail; bear to the right and cycle around it. Turn left on Cat Gap Trail. Grogan Creek is on your right.

Rosebay rhododendron flanking Long Branch Trail

7.8   At the fork in the trail, bear left onto the unmarked trail and pedal toward the forest-service road. The right (lower) fork is for hikers.

8.1   Turn left onto the forest-service road. (To the right is Robert's Bridge over Grogan Creek. The bridge leads to a trail back to the fish hatchery; this trail is for foot travel only.)

8.2   Enter the parking lot behind the fish hatchery. Cycle around the buildings and the fish pools.

8.5   You will arrive back at the main fish hatchery parking lot.

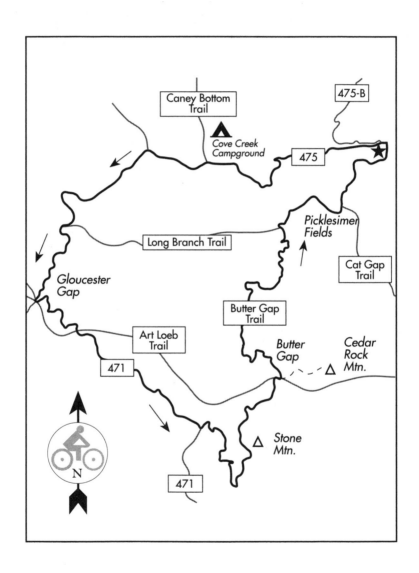

Fish Hatchery / Gloucester Gap / Butter Gap Trail Loop

Distance: 11.6 miles

Difficulty: Moderate

Riding surface: Gravel road, dirt road, single-track

Maps: 1. USGS 7.5 minute quadrangle, Shining Rock
      2. Pisgah District Trail Map

Access: From the ranger station, proceed north on U.S. 276 for 3.5 miles to the junction with F.R. 475 (Davidson River Road). Proceed 1.5 miles to the Pisgah Forest Fish Hatchery parking lot.

Elevation change: This ride begins at an elevation of 2,400 feet at the fish hatchery. It climbs to 3,200 feet at Gloucester Gap and reaches a maximum of 3,400 feet on F.R. 471 (Cathey's Creek Road). It then descends to 3,200 feet and climbs once more for 100 feet to Butter Gap. From Butter Gap to the fish hatchery, there is no elevation gain. The total elevation gain is 1,100 feet.

Season: The section of Butter Gap Trail which runs through Picklesimer Fields is closed to mountain bikes from April 15 to October 15. Therefore, this loop should be considered a winter ride.

View from Cedar Rock Mountain

This loop begins at the fish hatchery and follows F.R. 475, a climbing, narrow dirt road that parallels the Davidson River as it spills frothily over smooth, black rocks on its winding path down the mountain. This river is probably one of the most beautiful and pristine trout streams in western North Carolina. Fishermen come from far and wide to plant themselves in the cold river eddies and snap their fly rods in hopes of filling their baskets with a few rainbow trout or brookies.

By the time you cycle breathlessly into Gloucester Gap, the ascent is nearly over. Turn left onto F.R. 471 and climb for about 0.5 mile more. The grade moderates and then offers a welcome respite—a descent. This scenic, secluded dirt road leads to an unmarked trail on your left at about 7 miles. This trail is a sunny, grassy, old logging road that leads up to Butter Gap. At Butter Gap, there is a hiking trail which climbs to the bald granite top of Cedar Rock Mountain. The hike is strenuous but worth the effort, as it offers spectacular views of Kagle Mountain, Stone Mountain, Chestnut Mountain, Rich Mountain, and the entire Davidson River Valley. This trail is very dangerous when wet; hike only in dry weather.

Hop back on your bike after your hiking excursion and begin descending Butter Gap Trail. There is a cascading waterfall on the right festooned with lush hemlocks, rhododendron, and ferns. You will leave the forest and enter an open meadow known as Picklesimer Fields as you head toward the end of the ride. Grogan Creek, with its rushing white water, is on the right just before you cycle down to the fish hatchery parking area.

0.0 From the fish hatchery parking lot, cycle out to F.R. 475 and turn left.

0.2 At the fork, take the road to the left, F.R. 475. (F.R. 475B is on the right.)

2.6 To the right is a gated road that leads to Daniel Ridge Trail. Continue straight.

4.1 Long Branch Trail is on the left. Continue straight.

4.7 You will arrive at Gloucester Gap, an intersection of several roads and trails. Turn left onto F.R. 471.

5.4 Art Loeb Trail (foot travel only) crosses F.R. 471.

5.5 An unmarked, gated logging road is on the right; continue straight.

6.1 An unmarked, gated logging road is on the left; continue straight.

6.9 An unmarked trail begins at the gated logging road on the left. Turn left and pedal around gate. Begin a gentle climb on a grass road.

7.5 You will reach a rusted, open gate. Continue straight on the grass trail.

7.8 Art Loeb Trail crosses trail; continue straight.

8.0 You will arrive at Butter Gap. Turn left onto Butter Gap Trail and follow the blue blaze.

9.7 A cascading waterfall is on the right.

10.1 There is an intersection of trails. Long Branch Trail begins on the left, while Butter Gap Trail bears right. Follow Butter Gap Trail to the right across Picklesimer Fields.

10.6 You will reach an intersection with Cat Gap Trail; continue straight. Cycle around the large granite rock in the trail. Grogan Creek is on the right. Turn left onto Butter Gap Trail.

10.9 At the fork in the trail, bear left onto the unmarked trail and pedal toward the forst service road. The right (lower) fork is for hikers only.

11.3 Turn left onto the forest service road. (To the right is Robert's Bridge over Grogan Creek. The bridge leads to a trail to the fish hatchery; this trail is for foot travel only.)

11.6 You will arrive back at the fish harchery parking lot.

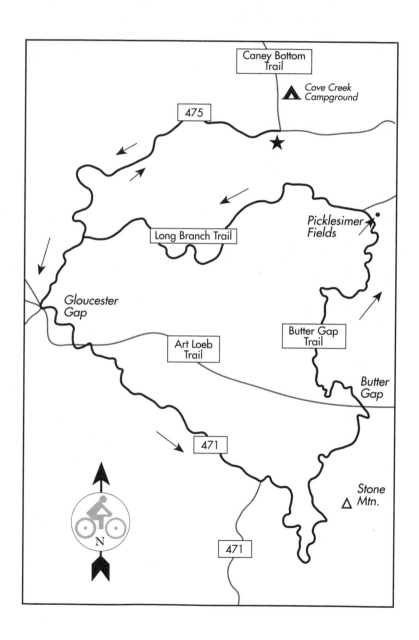

Caney Bottom Trail

Cove Creek Campground

475

Long Branch Trail

Picklesimer Fields

Gloucester Gap

Art Loeb Trail

Butter Gap Trail

Butter Gap

471

Stone Mtn.

N

471

Cove Creek / Gloucester Gap / Butter Gap Trail / Long Branch Trail Loop

Distance: 13.2 miles

Difficulty: Moderate

Riding surface: Gravel road, dirt road, single-track

Maps: 1. USGS 7.5 minute quadrangle, Shining Rock
2. Pisgah District Trail Map

Access: From the fish hatchery, drive 0.2 mile to the fork in the road. Bear left onto F.R. 475 (Davidson River Road). Cove Creek Campground will be on the right at 1.9 miles. A parking area is located on the left.

Elevation change: The ride begins at an elevation of 2,600 feet outside Cove Creek Group Campground. It climbs to a maximum of 3,400 feet on F.R. 471 (Cathey's Creek Road) just past Gloucester Gap. The elevation drops slightly and then climbs 100 feet at the approach to Butter Gap. Next, the ride drops to 2,800 feet before climbing to 3,100 feet on Long Branch Trail. The elevation then drops back to 2,600 feet on the return to the Cove Creek parking area. the total elevation gain is 1,200 feet.

Season: This loop is open year-round to mountain bikes.

Thisexcellent loop begins on F.R. 475 at the parking area outside Cove Creek Group Campground. This sylvan dirt road sculpts a path through exceptionally beautiful surroundings, with mountain springs, hemlocks, laurel, rhododendron, and mixed hardwoods contributing to the lushness of the setting. The arduous climb to Gloucester Gap continues for another 0.5 mile on F.R. 471 and then ends on a level grade, a welcome relief for panting cyclists. This rustic road winds through verdant forest on its way to an unmarked, grassy trail located on the left at about 5 miles; this wide-open, sunny trail is adorned with blackberry bushes that are heavy with dark, juicy berries in late summer.

At Butter Gap, you will turn left to begin a descent past a cascading waterfall, across cold mountain streams, and over open meadows warmed by sunshine. You will then turn left on Long Branch Trail and cross Searcy Creek almost immediately. A brief, steep, technical ascent follows in a heavily wooded section of trail. Next, the trail spills into a grassy meadow at about 9 miles and turns left to climb a steep bank. You will see a short spur trail leading to McCall Cemetery about 1 mile later. Cycle 250 yards to view the primitive tombstones, which rest idyllically on top of the ridge as a testimony to the colony of mountain settlers who lived in this area in the early 1800s. Retrace your path to Long Branch Trail and cycle through a tunnel of rhododendron on an old log pull back to F.R. 475. Turn right and enjoy the last couple of miles down to the Cove Creek area.

0.0   Park in the area opposite the gated road leading to Cove Creek Group Campground. The ride to Gloucester Gap begins as you turn left onto F.R. 475.

2.8   An intersection of roads and trails marks Gloucester Gap. The climbing is almost over. Turn left on F.R. 471.

5.0   A gated, grassy logging road is on the left. Turn onto this unmarked trail and pedal around the gate. Begin a gentle climb on a grass road.

View from Cedar Rock Mountain

6.1 You will reach Butter Gap. Turn left onto Butter Gap Trail (blue blaze) to descend to Long Branch Trail.

8.2 There is an intersection of trails. Butter Gap Trail continues straight and is closed to mountain bikes from April 15 through October 15. Turn left onto Long Branch Trail to continue the loop.

10.9 Long Branch Trail ends at F.R. 475. Turn right and cycle back to your vehicle.

13.2 You will arrive back at the parking area outside Cove Creek Group Campground.

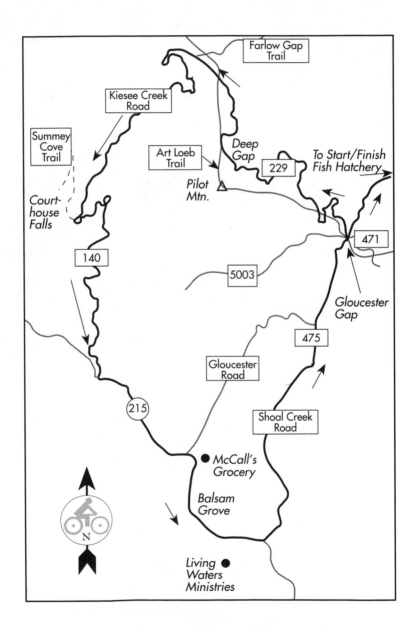

Farlow Gap Trail

Kiesee Creek Road

Summey Cove Trail

Courthouse Falls

Art Loeb Trail

Deep Gap

229

To Start/Finish Fish Hatchery

Pilot Mtn.

140

5003

471

Gloucester Gap

475

Gloucester Road

Shoal Creek Road

215

McCall's Grocery

Balsam Grove

Living Waters Ministries

N

Fish Hatchery / Gloucester Gap / Courthouse Falls / Balsam Grove / Shoal Creek Road Loop

Distance: 27 miles

Difficulty: Strenuous

Riding surface: Gravel road, dirt road, paved road, single-track

Maps: 1. USGS 7.5 minute quadrangle, Shining Rock
2. USGS 7.5 minute quadrangle, Sam Knob
3. USGS 7.5 minute quadrangle, Lake Toxaway
4. USGS 7.5 minute quadrangle, Rosman

Access: From the ranger station, proceed north on U.S. 276 for 3.5 miles to the junction with F.R. 475 (Davidson River Road). Proceed 1.5 miles to the Pisgah Forest Fish Hatchery parking lot.

Elevation change: This ride begins at 2,400 feet and climbs to a maximum elevation of 4,600 feet at Farlow Gap. A descent is then made to 2,800 feet at Balsam Grove, followed by an ascent to 3,200 feet at Gloucester Gap. The total elevation gain is 2,600 feet.

Season: This loop is open year-round to mountain bikes.

T his long ride leads serious cyclists on one of the best combinations of roads and trails in Pisgah National Forest. It offers a strenuous workout, panoramic views, and a number of highlights. During winter, Summey Cove Trail provides views of the Devil's Courthouse and Pilot Mountain. The Devil's Courthouse is a huge granite bald which, according to Cherokee legend, housed the courtroom of a giant, evil-eyed devil known as Judaculla.

The next highlight on this ride is a short hike down to Courthouse Falls, one of the prettiest waterfalls in western North Carolina. It is not a huge, thundering waterfall like some in the area, but it is truly splendid in its own right. The falls are located in a remote area of forest and drop about 80 feet into a still, deep pool. Courthouse Falls has such a celestial look that you almost expect to see gossamer-winged angels flitting about.

You will return to reality when you cycle into Balsam Grove on N.C. 215. Before leaving this small mountain hamlet, be sure to stop at McCall's Grocery Store for a Moon Pie, an RC Cola, and a chance to pet the hound dog sprawled out front. The owner of this small store is James McCall. He claims that about 80 percent of the folks in town are named McCall and that, of those 80 percent, more than half are named James. What the people of Balsam Grove lack in imagination, they make up for in hospitality—these are nice folks.

On Shoal Creek Road, you will pass Shoal Creek Baptist Church. A sign out front notes the name of the preacher: James McCall.

You will pass several Christmas-tree farms and well-kept homesteads as you wind back up to Gloucester Gap. The ride then loops back to the fish hatchery by descending on F.R. 475, a scenic dirt road bordered by a mixed forest of conifers, hardwoods, and rhododendron. It runs along the Davidson River—a sparkling mountain trout river—and is a perfect ending to an excellent day of mountain biking.

0.0 From the parking lot at the fish hatchery, cycle out to the stop sign and turn left.

0.2 At the fork in the road, bear left on F.R. 475.

4.7 You will arrive at an intersection of roads and trails at Gloucester Gap. Turn right on F.R. 229, a climbing gravel road. Click into your granny gear and mentally prepare yourself for the next several miles of relentless climbing.

6.2 There is a gated logging road to the right; bear to the left to continue.

6.9 The gravel road ends and a dirt road begins via a narrow, rocky, short trail access.

7.1 You will arrive at Deep Gap. The Deep Gap shelter is located off Art Loeb Trail, on the left. Continue straight.

7.2 There is an intersection of trails; take the trail to the right.

Christmas-tree farms abound on Shoal Creek Road.

Courthouse Falls

9.3 You will arrive at Farlow Gap. Continue straight at the intersection of trails. This trail will merge into Kiesee Creek Road.

10.5 A view of Pilot Mountain is to the left.

11.8 The road ends at a gate. Turn right onto F.R. 140 and descend on a screaming downhill to Summey Cove Trail. This descent is bittersweet when you consider that you will have to climb back up after viewing Courthouse Falls.

12.2 Turn left onto Summey Cove Trail.

12.4 A steep, short hiking trail on the left leads to Courthouse Falls. After a rest here, backtrack to F.R. 140. This road is washboard in sections. It parallels the lower end of the North Fork of the French Broad River.

14.7 Turn left onto N.C. 215 and cycle into Balsam Grove.

18.9 Turn left on the unmarked paved road across from Living Waters Ministries. There is a rock sign at the beginning of the road marked "Balsam Grove."

19.1 Turn left onto Shoal Creek Road.

21.1 Turn right onto F.R. 475.

22.3 Continue on F.R. 475 through Gloucester Gap toward the fish hatchery.

27.0 You will arrive back at your vehicle.

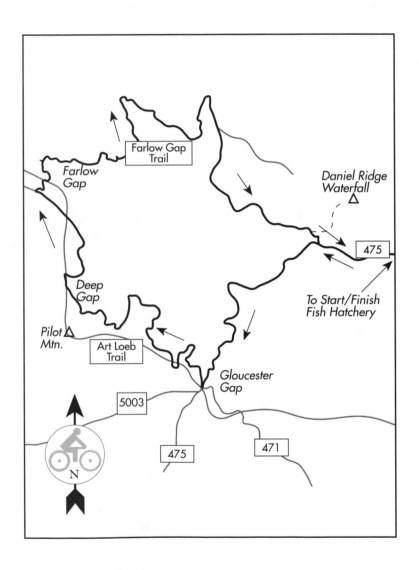

Farlow Gap
Trail

Farlow
Gap

Daniel Ridge
Waterfall
△

475

Deep
Gap

To Start/Finish
Fish Hatchery

Pilot △
Mtn.

Art Loeb
Trail

Gloucester
Gap

5003

475

471

N

Fish Hatchery / Gloucester Gap / Farlow Gap / Daniel Ridge Trail Loop

Distance: 17.6 miles

Difficulty: Strenuous

Riding surface: Gravel road, dirt road, single-track

Maps: 1. USGS 7.5 minute quadrangle, Shining Rock
2. Pisgah District Trail Map

Access: From the ranger station, proceed north on U.S. 276 for 3.5 miles to the junction with F.R. 475 (Davidson River Road). Proceed 1.5 miles to the Pisgah Forest Fish Hatchery parking lot.

Elevation change: You will begin at an elevation of 2,400 feet and climb to 3,200 feet at Gloucester Gap. The climbing continues to a maximum of 4,600 feet at Farlow Gap. From there, the elevation gradually decreases back to 2,400 feet as you approach the fish hatchery. The total elevation gain is 2,200 feet.

Season: This ride is open year-round to mountain bikes.

John Rock as viewed from the fish hatchery

This ride—with its grueling climbs, technical descents, and dangerous, precipitous drop-offs—is for serious cyclists only. You will begin on F.R. 475 and gradually climb to Gloucester Gap, which will give you an opportunity to warm your legs up for the serious climbing ahead. The road runs along the Davidson River, a scenic whitewater river popular with trout fishermen.

After arriving at Gloucester Gap, click into your granny gear and settle in for several miles of brutal climbing. There is a beautiful, panoramic view of the entire Davidson River Valley on the right just before Deep Gap. (If you are cycling with a group of expert cyclists who have strong moral convictions against resting, you might use this vista for the subject of a photograph and seize the chance to rest. I have found that "Kodak moments" are generally considered valid excuses for resting, even among hard-core cyclists. In fact, I often carry a camera with me on strenuous climbs. Most of the time, I don't even load it with film, but I click away just the same. That way, I can rest without being labeled a "weenie.")

At Farlow Gap, you will turn right onto Farlow Gap Trail. This single-track descends steeply in spots, is quite technical, and has serious, 100-foot drop-offs in sections. This trail should be ridden cautiously regardless of your experience. An old mica mine is visible after 0.5 mile as the trail winds around Shuck Ridge. The trail crosses Shuck Ridge Creek above some waterfalls and then snakes across the ridge in a set of sharp switchbacks which should be negotiated cautiously. It then follows Daniel Ridge, crosses Daniel Ridge Creek, and winds around the base of Fork River Ridge before intersecting with Daniel Ridge Trail.

Daniel Ridge Trail is a steep, technical descent which gradually moderates. It parallels Daniel Ridge Creek for most of its length. Once you reach the gravel road, 0.5 mile of cycling will lead you to a view of the Daniel Ridge Waterfall, which cascades over glistening ledges of dark granite. A final descent on the sun-dappled F.R. 475 will lead you back to the fish hatchery.

0.0 From the parking lot at the fish hatchery, cycle out to the stop sign and turn left.

0.2 At the fork in the road, bear left on F.R. 475.

4.7 You will arrive at an intersection of roads and trails at Gloucester Gap. Turn right on F.R. 229, a climbing gravel road.

6.2 There is a gated logging road to the right; bear left to continue.

6.9 The gravel road ends and a dirt road begins just beyond a short section of narrow, rocky single-track trail.

7.1 You will arrive at Deep Gap. The Deep Gap shelter is located off Art Loeb Trail, on the left. Continue straight.

Daniel Ridge Waterfall

7.2 There is an intersection of trails. Take the trail to the right.

9.3 You will arrive at Farlow Gap. Turn right.

13.1 Turn right onto Daniel Ridge Trail.

14.2 The single-track trail ends at a dirt road; continue straight.

14.8 The trail ends at a gravel road. Turn left to view the waterfall.

15.3 A view of the Daniel Ridge Waterfall is on the left. Retrace your path to continue.

16.1 Turn left onto F.R. 475.

17.6 You will arrive back at the fish hatchery.

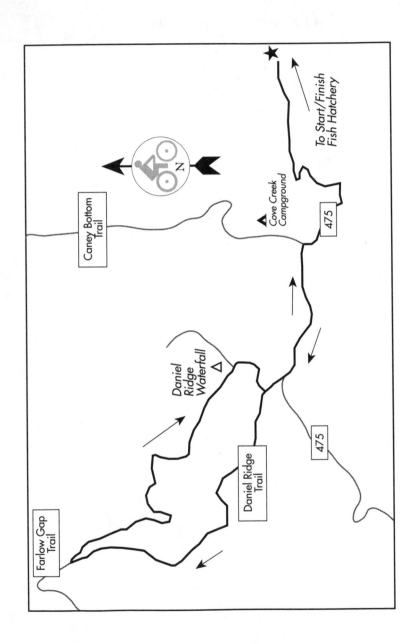

Farlow Gap Trail

Caney Bottom Trail

Daniel Ridge Waterfall

Daniel Ridge Trail

475

475

Cove Creek Campground

To Start/Finish Fish Hatchery

N

Daniel Ridge Trail Loop

Distance: 9 miles

Difficulty: Strenuous

Riding surface: Single-track, logging roads

Maps: 1. USGS 7.5 minute quadrangle, Shining Rock
2. Pisgah District Trail Map

Access: From the ranger station, proceed north on U.S. 276 for 3.5 miles to the junction with F.R. 475 (Davidson River Road). Proceed 1.5 miles to the Pisgah Forest Fish Hatchery parking lot.

Elevation change: The ride begins at the fish hatchery, which has an elevation of 2,400 feet. It reaches a maximum of 3,400 feet after turning onto Daniel Ridge Trail. The total elevation gain is 1,000 feet.

Season: This loop is open year-round to mountain bikes.

Daniel Ridge Trail parallelling Daniel Ridge Creek

Daniel Ridge Trail offers a good overall mountain-biking experience: a heart-pounding ascent, a technical descent, and scenery that rates as spectacular. The ascent is so steep and rocky in spots that dismounting and walking are necessary. However, the Davidson River, to the left of the trail, makes this push well worth the trouble. Churning white water and cascades tumbling over 15- to 20-foot drops will make you wish for your camera if you have left it at home. The trail levels off at about 4 miles and begins a descent. There are a few more climbs, but the trail is mostly level or descending at this point. Finally, just before you head back to your vehicle, a short optional excursion can lead you to the Daniel Ridge Waterfall, which delicately cascades over 200 feet of granite. After heavy rains, this fall becomes extraordinarily beautiful.

0.0   From the fish hatchery, cycle across the bridge over the Davidson River and turn left at the stop sign. You will immediately come to a fork in the road; take the road to the left, which is F.R. 475.

1.9   A road to the right leads to Cove Creek Group Campground. Continue straight.

2.6   A gravel parking area and a gated logging road are on the right. Turn right here. Go around the gate to get on the old gravel logging road.

2.7   You will cross the Davidson River on a concrete bridge. The scenery here is breathtaking.

2.8   Just before the logging road swings to the right, Daniel Ridge Trail is on the left. The trail is well-signed and blazed in red.

3.8   A log bridge is on the left. Bear right and climb. Less than half a mile up, you will reach the confluence of Daniel Ridge Creek and the Davidson River on the left. Turn right, follow the red blaze, and climb or push your bike.

4.5 The trail intersects with Farlow Gap Trail; turn right and follow the red blazes.

5.0 At the fork, bear right.

5.2 Cross a stream via a wooden footbridge.

5.4 A nice view of Looking Glass Rock is on the left. You will be pedaling (or walking!) a technical descent at this point.

5.5 The trail bends to the left.

5.6 The trail crosses a gravel road; continue straight.

5.9 You will pedal past two meadows along this stretch of trail.

6.1 You will cross several wooden bridges.

6.4 The top of Daniel Ridge Waterfall is on the left.

6.6 A rock outcropping is on the right. The trail makes a hard left turn.

6.8 The trail ends at the gravel road. Turn left and pedal a short distance if you wish to see the waterfall. Then retrace your path and pedal down the gravel road toward F.R. 475 (Davidson River Road).

7.2 Daniel Ridge Trail is on the right. Continue straight across the concrete bridge.

7.4 Turn left onto F.R. 475.

10.0 Return to the fish hatchery.

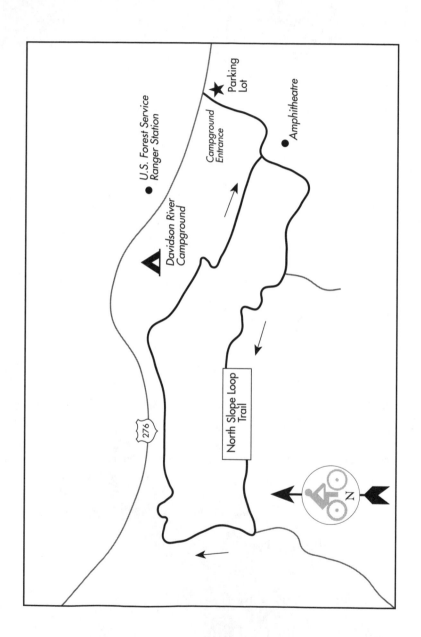

U.S. Forest Service
Ranger Station

Davidson River
Campground

Campground
Entrance

Parking
Lot

Amphitheatre

276

North Slope Loop
Trail

N

North Slope Trail Loop

Distance: 3.5 miles

Difficulty: Easy

Riding surface: Single-track

Maps: 1. USGS 7.5 minute quadrangle, Shining Rock
2. Pisgah District Trail Map

Access: From the ranger station, proceed south on U.S. 276 for 0.25 mile to the entrance to Davidson River Campground. Turn right and park in the Art Loeb trailhead lot, which is on the left.

Elevation change: The trail begins at 2,200 feet and gradually climbs to a maximum of 2,400 feet. It maintains this elevation until the end of the ride, where it drops again to 2,200 feet. The total elevation gain is 200 feet.

Season: This loop is open to mountain bikes from October 15 through April 15, so it should be considered a winter ride.

Lush foliage along the Davidson River

This easy loop is an excellent trail for beginners, though it is also ridden by experienced cyclists because of its outstanding trail condition and its proximity to Davidson River Campground.

This orange-blazed trail begins by passing the amphitheater and following an old logging road which meanders across the northern side of North Slope Ridge as it threads its way through a hardwood forest toward the Davidson River. The trail cuts through stands of rhododendron, laurel, and mature hemlock trees to find the river. Once there, it widens and follows an old railroad bed for about 0.5 mile. Turn right before cycling onto Exercise Trail, which is closed to mountain bikes year-round; return to the parking area on this leg of the loop.

0.3 From the Art Loeb Trail Parking lot, cycle past the campground's entrance booth and through the paved parking lot on the left. The trail begins on the gravel road to the amphitheater. At the fork in the trail, bear to the right and continue on the orange-blazed trail. It leaves the woods and continues briefly on the road, then returns to the woods as single-track.

0.4 Bear right at the fork in the trail. The trail begins a moderate climb.

0.5 There is an intersection of trails; take the right trail. Then take an immediate left turn; a steep climb follows for 0.2 mile.

2.3 A spur leading to North Slope Connector Trail (no bikes) is on the left. Turn right and continue on North Slope Trail.

3.1 Bear to the right at the intersection of trails. The river is on the left. The trail widens and follows and old logging road.

3.5 Exercise Trail is straight ahead; it is off-limits to mountain bikes year-round. Bear to the right to continue.

3.6 You will reach an intersection of trails. A historic cemetery is to the right; a campground is to the left. Continue straight.

4.6 You will arrive back at the parking area.

Davidson River

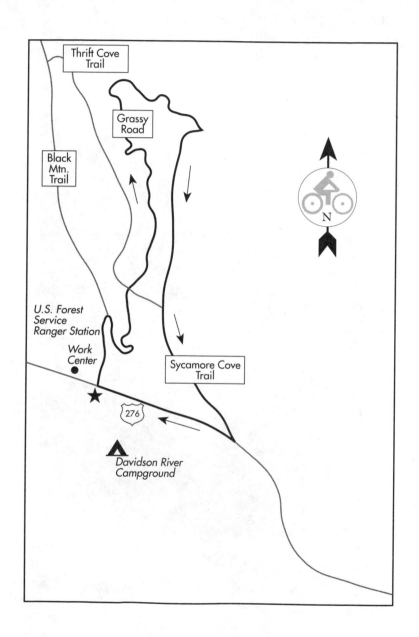

Thrift Cove Trail

Grassy Road

Black Mtn. Trail

U.S. Forest Service Ranger Station

Work Center

Sycamore Cove Trail

276

Davidson River Campground

N

Grassy Road /
Sycamore Cove Trail Loop

Distance: 3.2 miles

Difficulty: Easy

Riding surface: Logging road, single-track, short section of paved road

Maps: 1. USGS 7.5 minute quadrangle, Shining Rock
2. Pisgah District Trail Map

Access: From the ranger station, proceed south on U.S. 276 for 0.1 mile. Turn left into the large, paved parking area next to the work center. Park here, but stay outside of the security fence.

Elevation change: The ride begins at an elevation of 2,100 feet and gradually ascends to a maximum of 2,600 feet at the intersection with Sycamore Cove Trail. The total elevation gain is 500 feet.

Season: This loop is open year-round to mountain bikes.

Mushrooms are prolific in the damp, dark forest.

Snow occasionally covers the trails.

This short loop makes an ideal ride for beginning mountain bikers. Experienced riders looking for a short early-morning or late-afternoon ride will find it enjoyable as well.

The loop begins by climbing Grassy Road, an open logging road with no tree canopy to offer shade on hot summer days. It then turns onto Sycamore Cove Trail, a scenic single-track which begins on a level grade and then descends through groves of hemlocks on an old logging skid trail. The trail is easy overall, though there are steep sections near the end that will test your technical skills.

0.0 From the parking lot, turn left onto Black Mountain Trail which runs behind the work center.

0.2 Black Mountain Trail turns left, while Thrift Cove Trail bears to the right. Follow Thrift Cove Trail.

0.4 Grassy Road begins.

1.6 Grassy Road ends in a wildlife clearing lined with white pine trees. There are two trails on the far end of the clearing. Take the trail on the right, which is the west prong of Sycamore Cove Trail.

2.3 There is an intersection of trails. Mountains-to-Sea Trail goes to the right; continue on Sycamore Cove Trail, which makes a hard left turn.

2.9 The trail ends on U.S. 276; turn right to return to the parking lot.

3.2 You will arrive back at the parking lot.

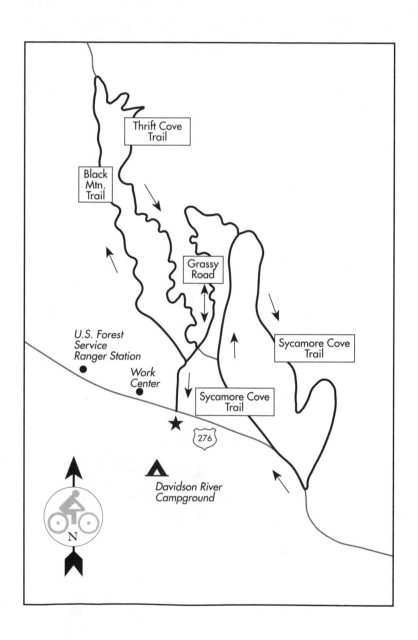

Thrift Cove
Trail

Black
Mtn.
Trail

Grassy
Road

U.S. Forest
Service
Ranger Station

Work
Center

Sycamore Cove
Trail

Sycamore Cove
Trail

276

Davidson River
Campground

N

Black Mountain Trail / Thrift Cove Trail / Sycamore Cove Trail / Grassy Road Loop

Distance: 9.9 miles

Difficulty: Moderate

Riding surface: Single-track, logging roads

Maps: 1. USGS 7.5 minute quadrangle, Pisgah Forest
        2. Pisgah District Trail Map

Access: From the ranger station, proceed south on U.S. 276 for 0.1 mile. Turn left into the large, paved parking area next to the work center. Park here, but stay outside of the security fence.

Elevation change: The loop begins at 2,100 feet and climbs to a maximum elevation of 2,800 feet at the junction of Black Mountain Trail and Thrift Cove Trail. The ride drops again to 2,100 feet at U.S. 276 before climbing to 2,600 feet on Sycamore Cove Trail. It then descends on Grassy Road back to the parking lot. The total elevation gain is 1,200 feet.

Season: This loop is open year-round to mountain bikes.

This is an excellent loop which lets you sample a number of popular mountain-biking trails. The loop begins on Black Mountain Trail, which throws you right into the teeth of some hard-core climbing. The trail ascends through a beautiful forest of mixed hardwoods, hemlock, rhododendron, and laurel. A trickling stream parallels the trail, and a cascading waterfall is off to the right at about 1 mile.

At the base of Little Hickory Knob, you will turn right onto Thrift Cove Trail and begin a descent on a winding logging road. You will have to climb again after you turn left onto Grassy Road, an open logging road which is hot during the summer months because of its lack of tree canopy. At the end of this road, you will enter a clearing lined with pines; both prongs of Sycamore Cove Trail are located at the far end of the clearing. Take the east prong, on the left. You will enter a dark, cool forest which is a stark contrast to the logging road you have just been cycling. This trail climbs for a short distance and then begins descending. The trail condition is excellent, though some technical skill is required in sections.

Mountain bikes are the new critters in the woods.

Streams and creeks abound in Pisgah National Forest.

The trail empties onto U.S. 276; turn right to pick up the west prong of Sycamore Cove Trail, located less than 0.25 mile up the road. You will cycle this single-track on a gently ascending grade for about 1 mile until the intersection with Grassy Road. Turn left and pedal the last few miles down to the parking lot.

0.0 From the parking lot, turn left onto Black Mountain Trail which runs behind the work center.

0.2 Turn left onto Black Mountain Trail. You will begin to climb immediately.

0.4 Mountains-to-Sea Trail is off to the right. Continue straight.

1.0 A cascading waterfall is to the right.

Sycamore Cove Trail

1.3 There is an intersection of trails; Black Mountain Trail turns left, while Thrift Cove Trail goes straight ahead. Follow the red-blazed Thrift Cove Trail.

3.4 At the intersection of trails, turn left onto Grassy Road, which is marked with an orange blaze.

4.6 Grassy Road ends in a pine-lined clearing. There are two single-track trails at the far end of the clearing. Take the trail on the left, which is the east prong of Sycamore Cove Trail. You will enter a dark forest whose floor is covered with ferns.

6.5 The trail ends at U.S. 276; turn right.

6.8 Turn right off U.S. 276 onto the west prong of Sycamore Cove Trail. This single-track is level for a short distance before it begins a moderate climb.

7.4 There is an intersection of trails. Mountains-to-Sea Trail goes straight; stay on Sycamore Cove Trail, which turns sharply to the right.

8.1 At the intersection, follow Grassy Road, which bears to the left.

9.3 Thrift Cove Trail is to the right; the Mountains-to-Sea Trail crosses it. Continue straight on Grassy Road to the parking lot.

9.9 You will arrive back at the parking lot.

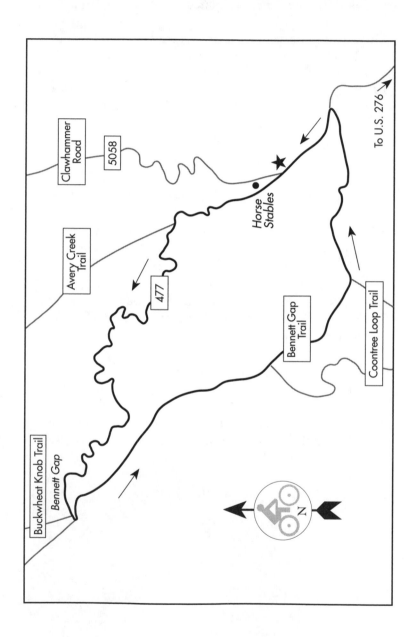

Clawhammer Road

5058

Avery Creek Trail

477

Horse Stables

Bennett Gap Trail

Coontree Loop Trail

Buckwheat Knob Trail

Bennett Gap

To U.S. 276

N

Avery Creek Road / Bennett Gap Trail Loop

Distance: 6.5 miles

Difficulty: Moderate to strenuous

Riding surface: Unpaved forest-service road, single-track

Maps: 1. USGS 7.5 minute quadrangle, Shining Rock
      2. USGS 7.5 minute quadrangle, Pisgah Forest
      3. Pisgah District Trail Map

Access: From the ranger station, proceed north on U.S. 276 for 0.6 mile to the junction with F.R. 477 (Avery Creek Road). Turn right onto F.R. 477 and drive 1.9 miles to a fork in the road near the horse stables. Park at the unpaved parking lot located here.

Elevation change: The loop begins at 2,400 feet and reaches its maximum elevation of 3,516 feet at Bennett Gap. The total elevation gain is about 1,100 feet.

Season: Bennett Gap Trail contains a section of Coontree Loop Trail which is open to mountain bikes only from October 15 through April 15, so this loop should be considered a winter ride.

Looking Glass Rock in winter

This loop begins with a moderate climb on F.R. 477, a shaded and scenic unpaved forest-service road. At Bennett Gap, you will begin riding on a single-track that follows a high ridge-line trail through open meadows. It descends south through Saddle Gap and along the eastern slope of Coontree Mountain. The final 2 miles of forest are typical of a creek-and-woodland trail.

From Bennett Gap Trail, there are good views of Looking Glass Rock, a scenic granite dome popular with rock climbers. During the winter when water freezes on the dome, it shines like an immense mirror. The Cherokee referred to it as the Devil's Looking Glass, possibly because it reflected an image of nearby Devil's Courthouse. A ride in midwinter, when the hardwood trees have lost all their leaves, offers the best views.

0.0 Begin from the parking area on the right side of F.R. 477. Go straight on F.R. 477 past the horse stables.

0.5 Lower Avery Creek Trail is on the right; continue straight.

0.8 Upper Avery Creek Trail is on the right; continue straight.

3.2 Bennett Gap Trail is on the left. Turn here. (A parking lot is located opposite the Bennett Gap trailhead.)

3.7 A great view of Looking Glass Rock is to the right. A very steep, technical descent follows. For most cyclists, this is a carry.

4.0 Perry Cove Trail intersects the trail from the left; continue straight.

4.4 Coontree Loop Trail, marked with a blue blaze, is on the right. This leg of Coontree Loop is closed year-round to mountain bikes. Continue straight on Bennett Gap Trail.

5.0 Coontree Loop Trail is on the right. This eastern leg of the trail is open seasonally to mountain bikes from October 15 to April 15. Continue straight on Bennett Gap Trail.

6.0 Turn left on Avery Creek Road.

6.5 Return to the parking lot at the horse stables.

Coontree Loop Trail

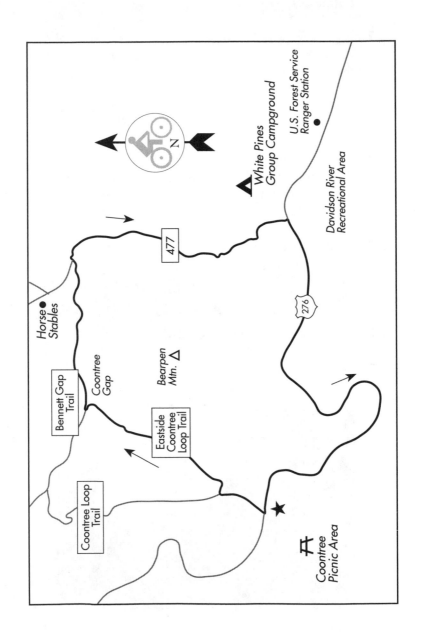

East-side Coontree Loop Trail /
Bennett Gap Trail /
Avery Creek Road Loop

Distance: 6.5 miles

Difficulty: Moderate

Riding surface: Single-track, gravel road, paved road

Maps: 1. USGS 7.5 minute quadrangle, Shining Rock
2. Pisgah District Trail Map

Access: From the ranger station, proceed north on U.S. 276 approximately 3 miles to Coontree Picnic Area, on the left. Park in the paved parking lot. The trail begins across the highway from the parking lot and is marked with a trailhead marker.

Elevation change: The loop begins at an elevation of 2,300 feet at Coontree Picnic Area and climbs to a maximum of 2,900 feet at the intersection with Bennett Gap Trail. From there, it descends back to an elevation of 2,300 feet at the intersection with F.R. 477 (Avery Creek Road) and follows a basically level grade back to the parking lot. The total elevation gain is 600 feet.

Season: The east side of Coontree Loop Trail is open to mountain bikes only from October 15 through April 15, so this loop should be considered a winter ride.

Bennett Gap Trail

The ride begins on Coontree Loop Trail. At about 0.2 mile, the trail forks; take the right fork, which is the east side of the trail. It is actually an old roadbed that parallels a trickling stream and passes through a glen of ferns and wildflowers on its climb to Coontree Gap. Bearpen Mountain, with a height of almost 3,400 feet, looms to the right.

At Coontree Gap, the trail intersects with Bennett Gap Trail; turn right and descend through a hardwood forest to F.R. 477. You will cross several pretty creeks on this descent. Turn right onto F.R. 477 (Avery Creek Road) and cycle 1.4 miles to U.S. 276. Turn right to return to the parking area.

0.0 The trail begins on level terrain. A babbling creek is on the left. In season, wildflowers are prolific at the beginning of this trail.

0.2 A wooden footbridge crosses the creek. There is a fork in the trail; take the right fork, which is the east side of Coontree Loop Trail. The west leg of Coontree Loop Trail is closed year-round to mountain bikes.

1.2 You will reach Coontree Gap and the intersection with Bennett Gap Trail. Turn right and begin a descent.

2.2 The trail intersects with F.R. 477; turn right.

3.6 F.R. 477 intersects with U.S. 276; turn right to return to the parking lot at Coontree Picnic Area.

6.1 You will arrive back at the Coontree parking lot.

Coontree Loop Trail

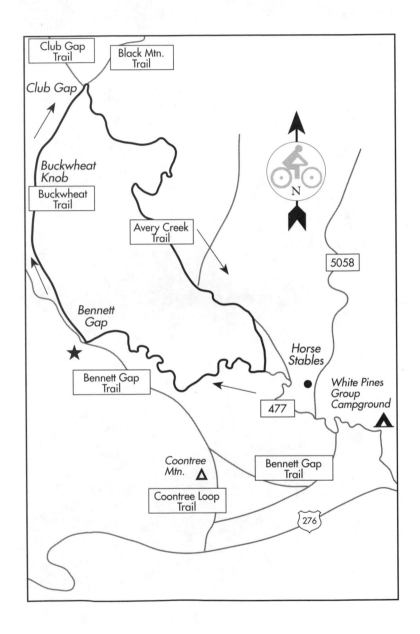

Buckwheat Knob / Avery Creek Trail Loop

Distance: 7.2 miles

Difficulty: Moderate

Riding surface: Single-track, dirt road

Maps: 1. USGS 7.5 minute quadrangle, Shining Rock
2. Pisgah District Trail Map

Access: From the ranger station, proceed north on U.S. 276 for 0.5 mile to the junction with F.R. 477 (Avery Creek Road). Turn right, drive 5.0 miles to Bennett Gap, and park opposite the trailhead.

Elevation change: The loop begins at 3,400 feet and ascends to a maximum elevation of 4,000 feet at Buckwheat Knob. From there, it descends to 2,600 feet at F.R. 477. It then climbs back up to the parking lot at 3,400 feet. The total elevation gain is 1,400 feet.

Season: This ride is open year-round to mountain bikes.

his loop begins on Buckwheat Trail, a steep climb that will get your heart rate up in a hurry. It passes through hardwood forests and grassy clearings as it makes its grueling way up to Buckwheat Knob. A descent leads to an intersection of trails. There, you will turn right onto Avery Creek Trail, which descends on an old roadbed as it passes through Club Gap and along the banks of Avery Creek. On this trail, you will cycle through an environment rich with typical creek-side flora, such as bluets, ferns, laurel, and hemlock. A number of small stream crossings add to a beautiful, thrilling descent.

0.0 Buckwheat Trail begins just past the parking lot on the right. Begin the climb to Buckwheat Knob and follow the yellow blaze.

0.3 You will reach a saddle or dip before the climb to the next knob begins.

0.7 You will reach the grassy summit of Buckwheat Knob. A descent follows.

1.6 There is an intersection of three trails. Black Mountain Trail goes straight to Buckhorn Gap; Club Gap Trail turns left to the Cradle of Forestry; and Avery Creek Trail turns right. Follow Avery Creek Trail as it begins a rocky, moderate descent.

The horse stables on F.R. 477

2.5 A new logging road which has been cut in this area crosses the trail at this point. Continue straight, follow the blue blaze.

3.2 There is a waterfall on the left.

3.9 You will reach an intersection with Buckhorn Gap Trail. Do not cross the creek. Bear right and follow the blue blaze of Avery Creek Trail.

4.0 At the fork, bear right on Upper Avery Creek Trail; the blaze changes to yellow.

4.9 Upper Avery Creek Trail ends at Avery Creek Road. Turn right and climb toward Bennett Gap.

7.2 You will return to the parking area at the Buckwheat Knob trailhead.

A level portion of F.R. 477

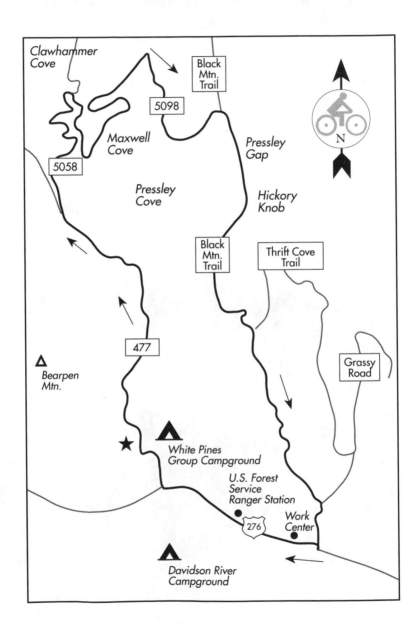

Clawhammer
Cove

Black
Mtn.
Trail

5098

Maxwell
Cove

Pressley
Gap

5058

Pressley
Cove

Hickory
Knob

Black
Mtn.
Trail

Thrift Cove
Trail

477

Grassy
Road

Bearpen
Mtn.

★

White Pines
Group Campground

U.S. Forest
Service
Ranger Station

Work
Center

276

Davidson River
Campground

N

Avery Creek Road / Pressley Gap / Black Mountain Trail Loop

Distance: 8.5 miles

Difficulty: Moderate

Riding surface: Dirt road, single-track

Maps: 1. USGS 7.5 minute quadrangle, Pisgah Forest
2. Pisgah District Trail Map

Access: Park in the spill-over parking lot next to the ranger station.

Elevation change: The ride begins at an elevation of 2,300 feet at White Pines Group Campground and climbs to a maximum of 3,400 feet at Hickory Knob on Black Mountain Trail. It then descends back to U.S. 276 and on to White Pines Group Campground. The total elevation gain is 1,100 feet.

Season: This loop of roads and trails is open year-round to mountain bikes.

A creek running alongside F.R. 477

This ride begins on F.R. 477, a rambling dirt road that crosses several pretty creeks on its way up to the intersection with F.R. 5058 (Clawhammer Road), a gated dirt road. After turning right on this road, you will climb up to F.R. 5098 (Maxwell Cove Road), where you will again turn right. Once on Maxwell Cove Road, settle back in your saddle, drop into your granny gear, and try to keep your cranks turning. This is, arguably, one of the toughest climbs in all of the Pisgah National Forest. You may find yourself praying for a flat tire, hoping to drop a chain, or wishing for any excuse under the sun to stop. But when you reach the crest of the mountain and turn your gaze southward, the fabulous view unfolding before you will make the agony of the climb well worth the effort. This dirt road climbs up the ridge to an intersection with Black Mountain Trail at Pressley Gap. There is one brief, final climb to contend with on Black Mountain Trail; you can rest at Hickory Knob before beginning the technical descent.

Black Mountain Trail passes through a mixed hardwood forest interspersed with evergreens such as laurel, rhododendron, and hemlock. Prior to the 1930s, this section of Pisgah National Forest was host to a tremendous stand of chestnut trees which was ultimately wiped out by a widespread blight.

Occasionally, a young chestnut seedling will spring up from the ground, only to soon wither and die.

The trail makes a technical descent through Thrift Cove on a rocky, old logging road. It ends at U.S. 276. Turn right on the highway and head toward F.R. 477, which leads back to White Pines Group Campground.

0.0 From the ranger station, turn right onto U.S. 276.

0.5 Turn right onto F.R. 477 (Avery Creek Road), an ungated dirt road.

2.4 You will reach a fork in the road near the horse stables. Bear right and pedal around the gate on F.R. 5058 (Clawhammer Road).

3.4 There is an intersection with another dirt road, F.R. 5098 (Maxwell Cove Road). Turn right here to climb to Pressley Gap.

5.9 The road intersects with Black Mountain Trail at Pressley Gap. Turn right onto Black Mountain Trail. You will come to a fork almost immediately; bear right and begin a technical descent.

6.9 Black Mountain Trail makes a screaming left turn. Continue to descend on a tight, technical path that leads to Thrift Cove Trail.

7.4 Turn left on Thrift Cove Trail. After a short climb, an incredible descent follows.

9.5 You will arrive at an intersection of Thrift Cove Trail and Grassy Road. Turn right onto Thrift Cove Trail and descend to U.S. 276.

10.0 Turn right onto U.S. 276.

10.3 Return to the ranger station.

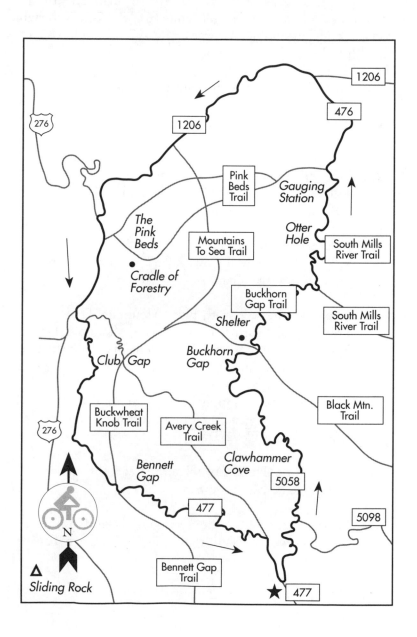

1206

476

1206

276

Pink Beds Trail

Gauging Station

The Pink Beds

Otter Hole

Mountains To Sea Trail

South Mills River Trail

Cradle of Forestry

Buckhorn Gap Trail

Shelter

South Mills River Trail

Club Gap

Buckhorn Gap

Buckwheat Knob Trail

Avery Creek Trail

Black Mtn. Trail

276

Bennett Gap

Clawhammer Cove

5058

5098

N

477

Bennett Gap Trail

477

Sliding Rock

Clawhammer Road /
Buckhorn Gap Trail /
South Mills River Trail /
Yellow Gap Road /
Avery Creek Road Loop

Distance: 19.1 miles

Difficulty: Strenuous

Riding surface: Single-track, dirt road, paved road

Maps: 1. USGS 7.5 minute quadrangle, Pisgah Forest
2. USGS 7.5 minute quadrangle, Shining Rock
3. USGS 7.5 minute quadrangle, Dunsmore Mountain
4. USGS 7.5 minute quadrangle, Cruso
5. Pisgah District Trail Map

Access: From the ranger station, proceed north on U.S. 276 for approximately 0.5 mile to F.R. 477 (Avery Creek Road). Turn right, drive 1.9 miles, and park at the parking area near the horse stables.

Elevation change: The ride begins at an elevation of 2,400 feet at the horse stables and reaches 3,400 feet at Buckhorn Gap. It descends to 3,200 feet at South Mills River Trail and then ascends to a maximum of 3,600 feet on F.R. 477 near Club Gap. The total elevation gain is approximately 1,400 feet.

Season: This loop is open year-round to mountain bikes.

Pink Beds Trail winding through a meadow

This loop of dirt roads and scenic, popular single-track trails will award serious cyclists with a full day of premium mountain biking. The ride begins on F.R. 5058 (Clawhammer Road), a gated dirt road behind the horse stables. It makes its way toward Buckhorn Gap via a serpentine climb through Clawhammer Cove; Black Mountain and Clawhammer Mountain can be seen on the right as you ascend.

After a long climb, you will turn right onto an unmarked logging road. Less than half a mile down, you will reach the intersection of Black Mountain and Buckhorn Gap Trails. This spot is a good place to rest for a few minutes and munch on an energy bar.

After turning left onto Buckhorn Gap Trail, a descent begins. (Hallelujah!) About a mile down the trail, you will reach a fork; bear right and stay on Buckhorn Gap Trail which is marked with an orange blaze. This portion of the ride is a moderately steep, technical descent. Watch for sandy sections that threaten to bring you down.

You also might watch for pigs. Yep, pigs. My friends and I spotted four feral hogs on one winter ride. From a distance, we thought the animals were dogs. But as we pedaled closer, we noticed tusks on the larger two of the critters. Instead of bolting for cover as we expected them to do, they begrudgingly moved to the edge of the trail to let us by. I suppose hog hunters don't ride mountain bikes.

When your computer has logged a little over 6 miles, you will reach another intersection of trails. Bear left on the high trail, South Mills River Trail. (If you turned right and pedaled about 1.5 miles, you would reach the Wolf Ford Suspension Bridge.) Almost immediately after bearing left on South Mills River Trail, you will reach another intersection of trails. Bear left again and begin a technical, rocky descent.

At about 8 miles, you will approach a gate which marks the terminus of South Mills River Trail. There is a spur trail to the left which leads to a water-level gauging station built in 1935. During the winter, you can turn left at the gauging station and cycle the north side of the Pink Beds Loop. The Pink Beds are an interesting wooded bog with moist, spongy ground. It is unusual for bogs to form at elevations as high as 3,200 feet. Because of the marshlike conditions, mountain bikers should avoid the Pink Beds after periods of heavy rain. It is believed that the name was derived from the dense growth of laurel and rosebay rhododendron, whose summer blossoms wash the area in the color pink. This optional trail is only open to mountain bikes from October 15 through April 15, while the south side of the Pink Beds Loop is closed to mountain bikes year-round.

Continue straight beyond the gate at the terminus of South Mills River Trail; you are now on F.R. 476 (Wolf Ford Road), which climbs to F.R. 1206 (Yellow Gap Road). Turn left on F.R. 1206, cycle to U.S. 276, turn left, and ride a short distance to the Cradle of Forestry, another interesting highlight open to visitors.

The Cradle of Forestry is a reconstruction of the first school of forestry in America. It sits on 6,400 acres of land designated by Congress in 1968 to commemorate this natural national historic site. The school was founded by Carl A. Schenck, a

German expert in forestry who was hired by George Vanderbilt to manage his thousands of forested acres. There are two easy loop trails for walking which tour the historic buildings of the Biltmore Forest School. The center is generally open from May through October and charges a nominal fee for admission. Check with the ranger station for hours.

From the Cradle of Forestry, continue south on U.S. 276 for about 0.5 mile before turning left on F.R. 477. The last climb of the ride begins. Buckwheat Knob can be seen on the left and is especially scenic during the winter season. After reaching Bennett Gap, you will find your hands gripping your brake levers during the screaming descent back to the parking area.

0.0 From one of the parking pull-offs near the horse stables, bear to the right and cycle around the gate on F.R. 5058. Prepare yourself mentally for the next 4.5 miles of climbing.

1.0 An unmarked grass road is on the right; continue straight.

2.5 Buckhorn Gap Trail, marked with an orange blaze, is on the left. Continue straight.

Crossing a foot log over the South Mills River

3.7 Buckhorn Gap Trail is on the left; continue straight.

4.0 Turn right onto an unmarked logging road.

4.3 Black Mountain Trail and Buckhorn Gap Trail intersect the logging road. Turn left onto Buckhorn Gap Trail and begin a descent. (Do not take the left that begins with a climb up crudely built steps; that is Black Mountain Trail.)

5.1 You will arrive at a fork in the trail; a grassy road climbs up the ridge on the left. Bear right and stay on Buckhorn Gap Trail.

Pink Beds Trail paralleling the South Mills River

6.2 You will arrive at an intersection of trails. Bear left on the high trail, South Mills River Trail. Almost imme-diately after bearing left, you will reach another intersection of trails. Bear left again and begin a technical, rocky descent.

6.7 Pedal across a concrete bridge that spans South Mills River.

8.0 South Mills River Trail ends. Continue straight on F.R. 476. (Note: If you choose the optional winter ride via the north side of the Pink Beds Loop, turn left here and follow the trail for 3.2 miles to U.S. 276. Turn left to pass the Cradle of Forestry and continue the loop. The ride will be shortened by 2 miles.)

9.3 Turn left at the intersection with F.R. 1206.

12.6 Turn left onto U.S. 276.

13.0 The Cradle of Forestry is on the left.

13.5 Turn left on F.R. 477 and begin the last climb of the ride.

15.9 The road intersects with Bennett Gap Trail at Bennett Gap. Continue straight on F.R. 477. There is a view of Coontree Mountain to the right.

19.1 You will arrive back at the horse stables.

North Mills River Area

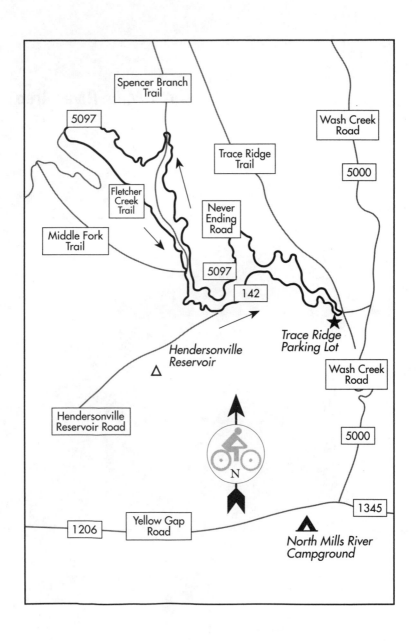

Spencer Branch Trail

5097

Wash Creek Road

5000

Trace Ridge Trail

Fletcher Creek Trail

Never Ending Road

Middle Fork Trail

5097

142

Trace Ridge Parking Lot

Hendersonville Reservoir

Wash Creek Road

Hendersonville Reservoir Road

5000

1345

1206

Yellow Gap Road

North Mills River Campground

N

Fletcher Creek Trail Loop

Distance: 9.2 miles

Difficulty: Easy to moderate

Riding surface: Gravel road, dirt road, single-track

Map: USGS 7.5 minute quadrangle, Dunsmore Mountain

Access: From I-26, take Exit 9 (the airport/Arden exit) and proceed west on N.C. 280 for 3.5 miles to the junction with N.C. 191. Drive south on N.C. 191 for 0.3 mile, then turn right on S.R. 1345 (North Mills River Road) at the North Mills River Recreation Area sign. Proceed 5 miles to the edge of the campground and turn right on F.R. 5000 (Wash Creek Road). Proceed 2 miles, bear left across the concrete bridge, and proceed 0.5 mile to the Trace Ridge parking area. Park here.

Elevation change: The ride begins at the parking lot at an elevation of 2,500 feet. It climbs along F.R. 5097 (Fletcher Creek Road) to a maximum elevation of 2,800 feet and then descends to 2,450 feet at Hendersonville Reservoir. It descends to 2,300 feet and then climbs back to 2,500 feet at the parking lot. The total elevation gain is 500 feet.

Season: This ride is open year-round to mountain bikes.

Fletcher Creek Trail

Whenever you ask a group of mountain bikers about their favorite trails in Pisgah National Forest, you are certain to hear Fletcher Creek Trail mentioned repeatedly. This popular trail affords mountain bikers of diverse abilities an excellent ride off the beaten track. Lush forest, gently rolling terrain, sunny meadows, and numerous creek crossings make this ride as scenic as it is fun.

The trail is accessed via F.R. 5097, which winds around the southern base of Coffee Pot Mountain before intersecting with the Fletcher Creek trailhead. After turning left, you will find a level trail which follows an old railroad grade for much of its length. The trail weaves through a forest of hemlocks, rhododendron, and hardwoods and crosses several wildlife clearings before intersecting with Spencer Branch Trail. The last leg of the trail becomes challenging and technical as it climbs a steep section and then plunges down a rocky descent. A left turn on F.R. 142 (Hendersonville Reservoir Road) will bring you back to the parking area.

0.0 The ride begins on F.R. 5097 (Never Ending Road), the gated road on the right of the parking lot. This winding, unpaved forest-service road gradually climbs to the trailhead. (It is the first gated road on the right as you drive into Trace Ridge parking lot.)

4.5 Spencer Branch Trail crosses the road. Continue straight.

5.5 The Fletcher Creek trailhead is on the left and is marked with a blue blaze. Turn here. Initially, the trail is quite wide; it immediately drops into a meadow, following a straightforward line.

6.8 There is an intersection of trails. Middle Fork Trail veers off to the right; continue straight to cross Fletcher Creek. (During cold weather, turn right on Middle Fork Trail for 300 yards, then take a left on the foot-log connector to stay dry while crossing the creek. Return upstream to the V-crossing and continue on Fletcher Creek Trail.) Spencer Branch Trail intersects Fletcher Creek Trail just past the creek crossing. Bear left on the blue-blazed Fletcher Creek Trail and begin a moderate ascent.

7.9 The trail ends at F.R. 142 (Hendersonville Reservoir Road). Turn left to return to the parking area.

9.2 You will arrive back at the Trace Ridge parking area.

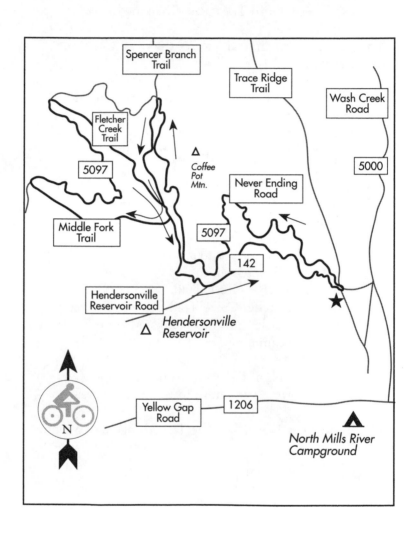

Spencer Branch
Trail

Trace Ridge
Trail

Wash Creek
Road

Fletcher
Creek
Trail

Coffee
Pot
Mtn.

5097

Never Ending
Road

5000

Middle Fork
Trail

5097

142

Hendersonville
Reservoir Road

Hendersonville
Reservoir

N

Yellow Gap
Road

1206

North Mills River
Campground

Spencer Branch Trail /
Middle Fork Trail /
Fletcher Creek Trail Loop

Distance: 12.7 miles

Difficulty: Moderate

Riding surface: Dirt road, single-track

Map: USGS 7.5 minute quadrangle, Dunsmore Mountain

Access: From I-26, take Exit 9 (the airport/Arden exit) and proceed west on N.C. 280 for 3.5 miles to the junction with N.C. 191. Drive south on N.C. 191 for 0.3 mile, then turn right on S.R. 1345 (North Mills River Road) at the North Mills River Recreation Area sign. Proceed 5 miles to the edge of the campground and turn right on F.R. 5000 (Wash Creek Road). Proceed 2 miles to the fork in the road. Bear to the left, cross the concrete bridge, and proceed 0.5 mile to the unpaved Trace Ridge parking area. Park here.

Elevation change: The loop begins at an elevation of 2,500 feet at the Trace Ridge parking lot and climbs to 2,800 feet on F.R. 5097 (Fletcher Creek Road) at the intersection with Spencer Branch Trail. It drops to 2,600 feet on Spencer Branch Trail and then climbs again on Middle Fork Trail. It reaches a maximum elevation of 3,000 feet on F.R. 5097 before descending on Fletcher Creek Trail. The elevation drops to 2,450 feet at Hendersonville Reservoir and continues to drop to a minimum of 2,300 feet. A final, brief climb back to the parking lot completes the ride. The total elevation gain is 900 feet.

Season: This loop of trails is open to mountain bikes year-round.

T his loop combines three of the most popular trails in the North Mills River area by connecting them with F.R. 5097. The road carves a meandering line along the base of Coffee Pot Mountain as it travels westward toward the trails. After turning left on Spencer Branch Trail, you will follow its gently descending line to an intersection of trails. There, you will pick up Middle Fork Trail and begin a moderate climb back up to F.R. 5097 along an old railroad grade; you will cycle across Middle Fork Creek and then enter a large meadow before reaching the road. Middle Fork Trail is frequently boggy and wet and should be avoided after periods of heavy rain to prevent trail damage and a mud bath.

The last single-track trail in this loop is Fletcher Creek Trail, which is accessed via F.R. 5097. You will turn right to descend this popular trail, which passes through three sizable, wildflower-studded meadows, across sparkling creeks, and down technical, rocky descents. It will lead you to F.R. 142 (Hendersonville Reservoir Road), where you will turn left to cycle back to the parking lot.

0.0 The loop begins on F.R. 5097 (Never Ending Road), the gated road on the right of the parking lot. This winding, unpaved forest road provides access to all three trails. (It is the first gated dirt road on the right as you drive in to Trace Ridge parking lot.)

4.5 The road intersects Spencer Branch Trail. Turn left here.

5.4 There is an intersection of trails. Turn right and cross Fletcher Creek. Almost immediately, turn left on the connector to Middle Fork Trail.

5.5 Turn right onto Middle Fork Trail.

6.8 Middle Fork Trail ends on F.R. 5097. Turn right and cycle toward the Fletcher Creek trailhead.

9.0 Turn right on Fletcher Creek Trail and descend toward the intersection of trails.

10.3 Cross Fletcher Creek and bear left at the intersection of trails to stay on Fletcher Creek Trail (marked with a blue blaze).

11.4 The trail ends at F.R. 142. Turn left to return to the parking lot. (Note: You can view Hendersonville Reservoir by turning right and cycling a short distance. Retrace your path and continue toward the parking lot to complete the loop.)

12.7 You will arrive back at the parking lot.

Pushing uphill on F.R. 5097

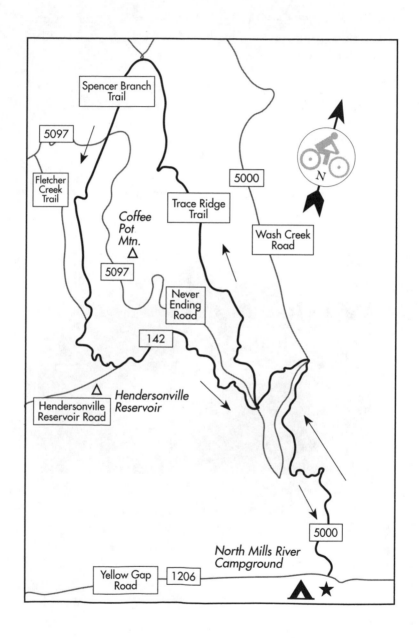

Wash Creek Road /
Trace Ridge Trail /
Spencer Branch Trail Loop

Distance: 12.0 miles

Difficulty: Strenuous

Riding surface: Dirt road, single-track

Map: USGS 7.5 minute quadrangle, Dunsmore Mountain

Access: From I-26, take Exit 9 (the airport/Arden exit) and proceed west on N.C. 280 for 3.5 miles to the junction with N.C. 191. Drive south on N.C. 191 for 0.3 mile, then turn right on S.R. 1345 (North Mills River Road) at the North Mills River Recreation Area sign. Proceed 5 miles to the edge of the campground and park in the paved parking lot on the left.

Elevation change: This ride begins at the campground at an elevation of 2,200 feet. It reaches a maximum of 3,200 feet at the intersection of Trace Ridge Trail and Spencer Branch Trail. It descends to 2,300 feet at F.R. 142 (Hendersonville Reservoir Road) and briefly climbs to 2,500 feet at the Trace Ridge parking lot. From there, it descends back to the campground. The total elevation gain is 1,200 feet.

Season: This ride is open year-round to mountain bikes.

Rounding a bend on F.R. 5097

The ride begins from the North Mills River campground on F.R. 5000 (Wash Creek Road), a gradually ascending dirt road which is a good warmup for the serious single-track climbing ahead. You will cycle into the Trace Ridge parking lot after a few miles and find the Trace Ridge trailhead at its northern end, just to the right of gated F.R. 5097 (Fletcher Creek Road). Trace Ridge Trail follows an old forest road on a level grade for a short distance and then turns left onto climbing single-track. It is steep, narrow, and rocky in sections.

The loop intersects with Spencer Branch Trail after a few more miles and begins an extremely steep, rocky, technical descent. The trail moderates after about 0.5 mile, crosses several gurgling streams, and snakes through an arbor of shiny green laurel. It then crosses F.R. 5097 and continues on a level course until intersecting with Fletcher Creek Trail. You will finish on Fletcher Creek Trail, which leads to F.R. 142. A left turn here will take you to the Trace Ridge parking lot and then return you to the campground.

0.0   From the campground, turn left on F.R. 5000 (Wash Creek Road).

2.0 Turn left on F.R. 142.

2.5 You will enter the Trace Ridge parking lot. The trail begins at the northern end of the lot, just to the right of gated F.R. 5097 (Never Ending Road). Several tank traps or berms are located at the trailhead.

2.8 There is a fork in the trail. Bear left and begin a steep, technical climb on a clay single-track trail.

5.0 A large, flat granite rock is embedded in the trail. You may have to walk your bike over it.

5.3 Trace Ridge Trail intersects with Spencer Branch Trail. Make a sharp left turn and begin a very steep, technical descent. Inexperienced riders should dismount and walk their bikes for this short section. (Another option is to turn right for a fantastic descent on Spencer Gap Trail and Wash Creek Road. The total mileage in this direction is 11.7 miles.)

6.1 The trail intersects with F.R. 5097 (Never Ending Road). Cross the road and continue straight on Spencer Branch Trail.

7.1 Spencer Branch Trail intersects with Fletcher Creek Trail; turn left and continue on Fletcher Creek Trail, marked with blue blazes.

8.2 The trail ends at F.R. 142 (Hendersonville Reservoir Road); turn left to return to the Trace Ridge parking lot.

9.5 You will arrive at the Trace Ridge parking lot.

10.0 Turn right on F.R. 5000.

12.0 You will arrive back at the North Mills River campground.

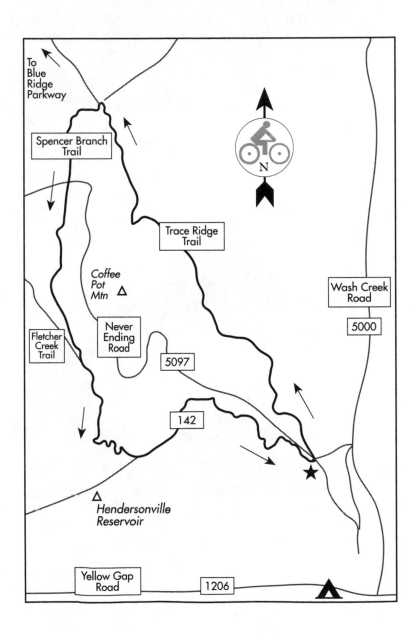

Trace Ridge Trail / Spencer Branch Trail Loop

Distance: 7.0 miles

Difficulty: Strenuous

Riding surface: Single-track, dirt road

Map: USGS 7.5 minute quadrangle, Dunsmore Mountain

Access: From I-26, take Exit 9 (the airport/Arden exit) and proceed west on N.C. 280 for 3.5 miles to the junction with N.C. 191. Drive south on N.C. 191 for 0.3 mile, then turn right on S.R. 1345 (North Mills River Road) at the North Mills River Recreation Area sign. Proceed 5 miles to the edge of the campground and turn right on F.R. 5000 (Wash Creek Road). Proceed 2 miles, bear left across the concrete bridge, and proceed 0.5 mile to the unpaved Trace Ridge parking area. Park here.

Elevation change: This ride begins at 2,500 feet and climbs to a maximum elevation of 3,200 feet at the junction with Spencer Branch Trail. The elevation drops to 2,800 feet at the junction with F.R. 5097 (Fletcher Creek Road) and descends to 2,300 feet on F.R. 142 (Hendersonville Reservoir Road). There is a brief climb back to 2,500 feet as you approach the parking lot. The total elevation gain is 900 feet.

Season: This ride is open year-round to mountain bikes.

T his loop of trails is the condensed version of the ride described in the previous chapter. If you need a shorter ride and don't mind starting right in the teeth of a hard-core technical climb, this ride offers an excellent alternative.

The loop begins from the Trace Ridge parking lot and follows a level, old logging road for a short distance before turning left onto climbing single-track. The narrow trail is steep and rocky in sections, which makes this a technical, difficult ascent. The trail follows a ridge line through a stand of maples, oaks, hickories, and white pines. Trace Ridge Trail is actually the old ridge road to the Blue Ridge Parkway. After almost 3 miles of climbing, it intersects with Spencer Branch Trail, where you will turn sharply to the left.

If you like thrills, you will love Spencer Branch Trail. It begins with a steep descent which requires advanced technical skill. The grade then moderates and crosses several pretty creeks. Early-morning rides on this trail are especially scenic, as eastern sunshine fills the forest, forming colonnades of soft light filtering through the trees. This narrow single-track trail descends for several more miles while skirting the base of Coffee Pot Mountain. The ride then continues on Fletcher Creek Trail until it meets F.R. 142. A left turn on this dirt road will take you back to the parking area.

0.0 Trace Ridge Trail begins at the northern end of the parking area just to the right of gated F.R. 5097 (Never Ending Road). Several tank traps or berms are located at the trailhead.

0.3 There is a fork in the trail; bear left and begin a steep, technical climb on a clay single-track trail.

2.5 A large, flat granite rock is embedded in the trail. You may have to walk your bike over it.

2.8 Trace Ridge Trail intersects with Spencer Branch Trail. Make a sharp left turn. Spencer Branch Trail starts off extremely steep and rocky. Some cyclists may find it necessary to dismount during this brief section.

3.6   The trail crosses F.R. 5097 (Never Ending Road) and continues straight.

4.6   The trail intersects with Fletcher Creek Trail; turn left onto Fletcher Creek Trail and head toward F.R. 142 (Hendersonville Reservoir Road).

5.7   Fletcher Creek Trail terminates at F.R. 142. Turn left and cycle up to the parking lot.

7.0   You will arrive back at the parking area.

Crossing Fletcher Creek

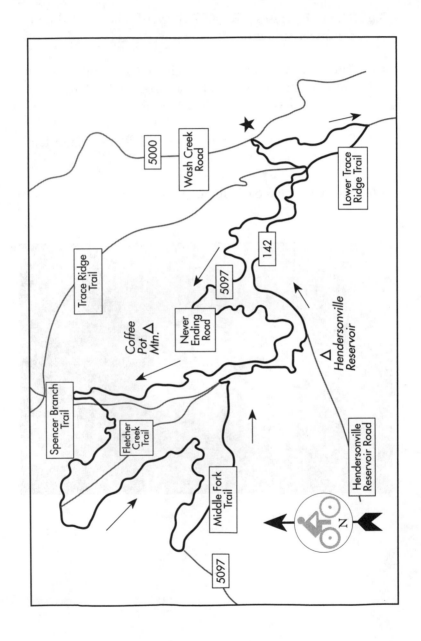

Wash Creek Trail /
Middle Fork Trail Loop

Distance: 13.4 miles

Difficulty: Moderate

Riding surface: Gravel road, dirt road, single-track

Maps: 1. USGS 7.5 minute quadrangle,
            Dunsmore Mountain
       2. Pisgah District Trail Map

Access: From I-26, take Exit 9 (the airport/Arden exit) and proceed west on N.C. 280 for 3.5 miles to the junction with N.C. 191. Drive south on N.C. 191 for 0.3 mile, then turn right on S.R. 1345 (North Mills River Road) at the North Mills River Recreation Area sign. Proceed 5 miles to the edge of the campground and turn right on F.R. 5000 (Wash Creek Road). Proceed 2 miles to the fork in the road and park at the pull-off on the right next to the gated road to the clearing.

Elevation change: The ride begins at an elevation of 2,500 feet at the parking area. It climbs to a maximum of 3,000 feet on F.R. 5097 (Fletcher Creek Road) just before dropping onto Middle Fork Trail. It descends to 2,450 feet at Hendersonville Reservoir and then to 2,300 feet. A final climb to 2,500 feet returns you to the parking area. The total elevation gain is 700 feet.

Season: This ride is open to mountain bikes year-round.

Middle Fork Creek

This is a fairly long ride which combines a dirt road with exceptionally beautiful single-track trail. It begins on a short section of single-track which will tease you into wanting more. The route continues on F.R. 5097, a scenic gravel road which gradually gains elevation while meandering along the base of Coffee Pot Mountain. Sections of this road are heavily canopied with tree branches from the surrounding forest, while other sections are wide-open, sunny, and punctuated with blue skies.

After about 9 miles, you will reach Middle Fork Trail and turn left onto descending single-track. The initial section of this single-track is wet and boggy almost all the time and should be avoided after heavy rains to prevent trail damage. After about 1 mile, Middle Fork Trail ends at the intersection of Fletcher Creek Trail and Spencer Branch Trail. Continue on Fletcher Creek Trail for a brief, steep climb before you descend on a rocky, technical section to F.R. 142 (Hendersonville Reservoir Road). At the road, turn left and pedal about 2 miles back to the parking area.

0.0 From the parking area, cross the bridge and turn left onto Wash Creek Trail which is mostly level single track.

1.0 Wash Creek Trail intersects with Trace Ridge Trail. Make a hard right and ride to the unpaved Trace Ridge parking lot.

1.4 At the parking lot, follow F.R. 5097 (Never Ending Road), which is the gated road on the far left.

5.9 Spencer Branch Trail crosses the road. Continue straight.

6.9 You will see the Fletcher Creek trailhead on the left side of the road. Continue straight.

9.1 Turn left on Middle Fork Trail and descend for the next mile.

10.4 At fork, bear left at sign "To Spencer Branch Trail."

10.5 Turn right; cross Fletcher Creek. Bear left and follow Fletcher Creek Trail (blue blaze).

11.6 The trail ends at F.R. 142 (Hendersonville Reservoir Road). Turn left to return to the parking lot. (Note: If you would like to see the reservoir, turn right and cycle 0.2 mile; retrace your path to complete the loop.)

12.9 Pass through the Trace Ridge parking area and descend to the parking area where you left your car.

13.4 You will arrive back at your vehicle.

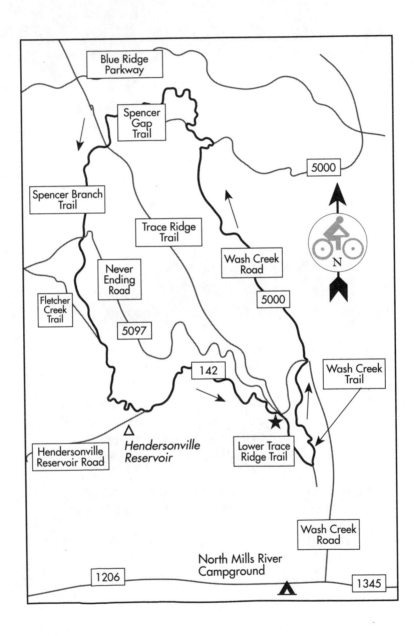

Blue Ridge
Parkway

Spencer
Gap
Trail

Spencer Branch
Trail

Trace Ridge
Trail

Wash Creek
Road

5000

Never
Ending
Road

Fletcher
Creek
Trail

5097

142

Wash Creek
Trail

Hendersonville
Reservoir Road

Hendersonville
Reservoir

Lower Trace
Ridge Trail

Wash Creek
Road

North Mills River
Campground

1206

1345

N

Wash Creek Trail / Wash Creek Road / Spencer Gap Trail / Spencer Branch Trail Loop

Distance: 9.5 miles

Difficulty: Strenuous

Riding surface: Dirt road, single-track

Maps: 1. USGS 7.5 minute quadrangle, Dunsmore Mountain
2. Pisgah District Trail Map

Access: From I-26, take Exit 9 (the airport/Arden exit) and proceed west on N.C. 280 for 3.5 miles to the junction with N.C. 191. Drive south on N.C. 191 for 0.3 mile, then turn right on S.R. 1345 (North Mills River Road) at the North Mills River Recreation Area sign. Proceed 5 miles to the edge of the campground and turn right on F.R. 5000 (Wash Creek Road). Proceed 2 miles, bear left across the concrete bridge, and proceed 0.5 mile to the unpaved Trace Ridge parking area. Park here.

Elevation change: The ride begins at an elevation of 2,500 feet and drops to 2,400 feet on F.R. 142 (Hendersonville Reservoir Road). It climbs to a maximum of 3,200 feet at the junction of Spencer Branch Trail and Trace Ridge Trail. It then drops to 2,300 feet before climbing back up to 2,500 feet at the parking lot. The total elevation gain is 1,000 feet.

Season: This loop is open year-round to mountain bikes.

This ride begins on the lower portion of Trace Ridge Trail. It soon intersects with Wash Creek Trail and continues an easy descent through heavy forest. A right turn on F.R. 142 will lead you to F.R. 5000, a lovely dirt road whose grade gradually increases to a moderately strenuous ascent. This laborious climb is sure to warm you up for the serious ascent on Spencer Gap Trail. Once on Spencer Gap Trail, you will come to a fork; turn right to begin the toughest climb of the ride. Though brief, it is sure to leave you breathless. Spencer Gap Trail then winds through Beaverdam Gap to the junction of Spencer Branch and Trace Ridge trails, where a memorable descent awaits you.

The first time I rode Spencer Branch Trail, I stood at the top and looked down at the steep descent wondering what the chances were of making it to the bottom with my collarbone still intact. Summoning all my courage, I sent up desperate prayers to the bicycling gods and then let her roll. With all my weight to the rear, I squeezed my saddle with my knees and scrubbed some speed with my rear brakes. I was terrified, but by the time I made it to the bottom, I was ready to climb back up and do it again. Thrill seekers take notice: If this descent doesn't send adrenaline coursing through your veins, then nothing will.

The ride is anticlimactic after crossing F.R. 5097 (Fletcher Creek Road), but it is still scenic and enjoyable. After another mile on Spencer Branch Trail, you will pick up Fletcher Creek Trail and cycle to F.R. 142. From there, you will climb back up to the parking lot to end the ride.

A sun-dappled portion of F.R. 5000

0.0 As you drive into the parking lot, the lower portion of Trace Ridge Trail will be on the far end of the parking lot. Begin here.

0.4 Make a hard left onto Wash Creek Trail.

1.4 Turn right onto F.R. 142.

1.5 Turn left onto F.R. 5000 (Wash Creek Road).

2.0 Bad Fork Trail (foot travel only) is on right.

3.5 Turn left onto Spencer Gap Trail, a gated grass road.

3.9 There is a fork in the trail; bear right and prepare to attempt a serious climb.

5.3 You will reach the intersection with Trace Ridge Trail. Turn left, pedal about 30 yards, then turn right on Spencer Branch Trail.

6.1 Spencer Branch Trail crosses F.R. 5097 (Never Ending Road). Continue straight on Spencer Branch Trail.

7.1 Turn left at the intersection with Fletcher Creek Trail. Follow the trail to F.R. 142 (Hendersonville Reservoir Road).

8.2 Turn left on F.R. 142.

9.5 You will arrive back at the Trace Ridge parking area.

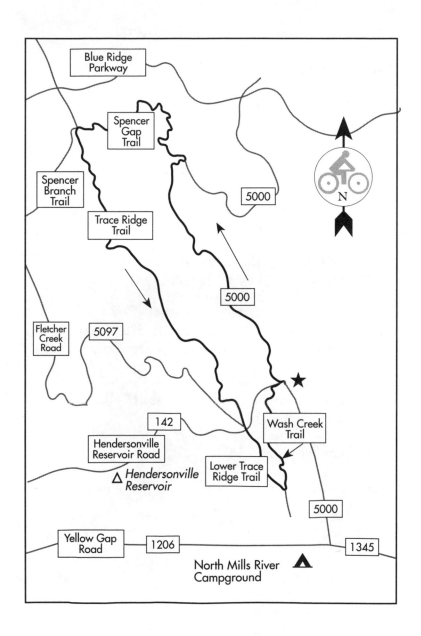

Wash Creek Road / Spencer Gap Trail / Trace Ridge Trail / Wash Creek Trail Loop

Distance: 8 miles

Difficulty: Moderate to strenuous

Riding surface: Dirt road, single-track

Maps: 1. USGS 7.5 minute quadrangle, Dunsmore Mountain
2. Pisgah District Trail Map

Access: From I-26, take Exit 9 (the airport/Arden exit) and proceed west on N.C. 280 for 3.5 miles to the junction with N.C. 191. Drive south on N.C. 191 for 0.3 mile, then turn right on S.R. 1345 (North Mills River Road) at the North Mills River Recreation Area sign. Proceed 5 miles to the edge of the campground and turn right on F.R. 5000 (Wash Creek Road). Proceed 2 miles to a fork in the road. Park at the pull-off next to the large, grassy clearing on the right. Do not block the gate.

Elevation change: The ride begins at an elevation of 2,400 feet at the parking area and climbs to a maximum of 3,200 feet at the junction of Spencer Branch Trail and Trace Ridge Trail. It descends back to 2,400 feet without any additional gain in elevation. The total elevation gain is 800 feet.

Season: This loop is open year-round to mountain bikes.

A stream-side section of F.R. 5000

Cycling an easy portion of F.R. 5000

The ride begins on a verdant dirt road which runs along Wash Creek for several miles. It follows a gently ascending grade that increases to a moderately strenuous climb as it approaches Spencer Gap Trail. Spencer Gap Trail begins as a narrow, gently climbing single-track, but once it intersects with a logging road and turns right, a strenuous climb ensues which will test your climbing abilities. Fortunately, the climb is not lengthy, and the trail soon levels out as it winds through Beaverdam Gap.

Spencer Gap Trail ends at the junction of Spencer Branch and Trace Ridge trails; continue straight on Trace Ridge Trail toward the parking area. This is a technical, steep, rocky descent that will test both your skills and your courage. Cross the parking lot and continue on the southern portion of Trace Ridge Trail until it intersects with Wash Creek Trail. Make a hard left on this single-track, which is covered with thick layers of pine needles. Descend until the trail ends at F.R. 142 (Hendersonville Reservoir Road). Turn right to return to your vehicle.

0.0 From the parking area, cycle up F.R. 5000, (Wash Creek Road.)

0.5 Bad Fork Trail (foot travel only) is on the right.

2.0 Turn left onto Spencer Gap Trail, a gated grass road.

2.4 There is a fork in the trail; bear right and climb a very steep hill.

3.8 You will reach the intersection with Trace Ridge Trail; turn left on Trace Ridge Trail. You will begin a descent.

6.6 You will cycle into the Trace Ridge parking lot. Cross the lot and continue on Lower Trace Ridge Trail.

7.0 Make a hard left turn onto Wash Creek Trail.

8.0 Turn right onto F.R. 142 to return to your vehicle.

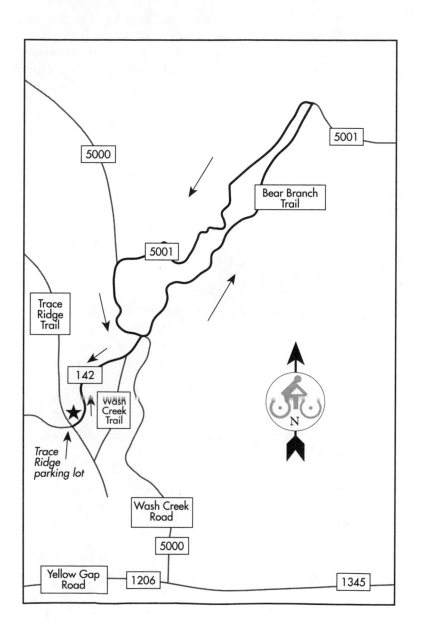

Bear Branch Trail Loop

Distance: 2.8 miles

Difficulty: Easy

Riding surface: Single-track, dirt road

Maps: 1. USGS 7.5 minute quadrangle,
Dunsmore Mountain
2. Pisgah District Trail Map

Access: From I-26, take Exit 9 (the airport/Arden exit) and proceed west on N.C. 280 for 3.5 miles to the junction with N.C. 191. Drive south on N.C. 191 for 0.3 mile, then turn right on S.R. 1345 (North Mills River Road) at the North Mills River Recreation Area sign. Proceed 5 miles to the edge of the campground and turn right on F.R. 5000 (Wash Creek Road). Proceed 2 miles to the fork in the road, bear left across a concrete bridge. Drive 0.5 mile to Trace Ridge parking lot; park here.

Elevation change: The ride begins at an elevation of 2,500 feet and gently ascends to a maximum of 2,800 feet. It then gradually descends to 2,400 feet as you cycle back to F.R. 5000. The total elevation gain is 500 feet.

Season: This ride is open year-round to mountain bikes.

Bear Branch Trail

This short, easy loop is an excellent ride for children and beginners. It can be lengthened to 6.8 miles by beginning at the campground and cycling up F.R. 5000 to the Bear Branch trailhead.

The ride begins on a wide, level single-track and parallels a large, grassy clearing on the right for a short distance. It enters a mixed forest of hardwoods and evergreens as it gently ascends along the western slope of Seniard Mountain. It then intersects with a dirt road for an easy, fun descent to F.R. 5000.

0.0 As you drive into the parking lot, the lower portion of Trace Ridge Trail will be on the far end of the parking lot. Begin here.

0.4 Make a hard left onto Wash Creek Trail.

1.4 Turn right onto F.R. 142.

1.5 You will reach F.R. 5000 (Wash Creek Road). The Bear Branch trailhead is almost straight ahead. Pedal around the gate to reach the blue-blazed trail.

3.6 Bear left at the fork in the trail.

3.7 At the intersection with the grass road, turn left.

3.9 Turn left on the dirt road.

4.4 Turn left on F.R. 5000 (Wash Creek Road).

4.8 Turn right on F.R. 142 and pedal across the concrete bridge.

5.3 Return to Trace Ridge parking lot.

Mountain stream

Pink Beds / South Mills River Area

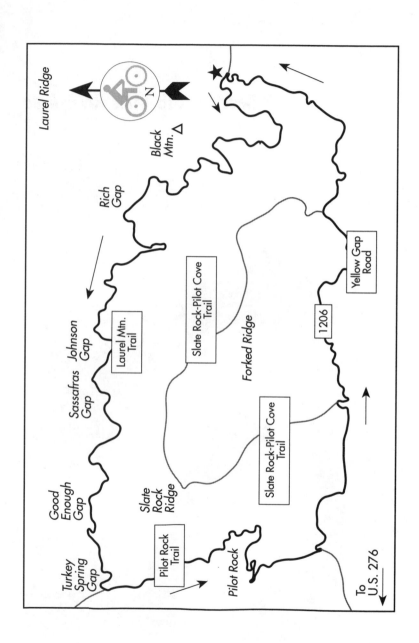

Laurel Mountain Trail / Pilot Rock Trail Loop

Distance: 13.8 miles

Difficulty: Moderate to strenuous

Riding surface: Single-track, dirt road

Maps: 1. USGS 7.5 minute quadrangle,
Dunsmore Mountain
2. Pisgah District Trail Map

Access: From the ranger station, proceed north on U.S. 276 for 11 miles to F.R. 1206 (Yellow Gap Road). Turn right and proceed 9 miles to Yellow Gap. Park here.

Elevation change: The ride begins at an elevation of 3,000 feet at Yellow Gap. It ascends quickly to a maximum of 4,800 feet at the connector between trails. From there, the trail descends to a minimum of 2,800 feet at F.R. 1206 and then climbs back to 3,000 feet at the parking area. The total elevation gain is 2,000 feet.

Season: This loop is open year-round to mountain bikes.

*Laurel Mountain Trail snaking its way
under a granite overhang*

This loop begins on a gradually ascending single-track trail which passes through Rich Gap, Johnson Gap, Sassafras Gap, Good Enough Gap, and finally along a ridge line to Turkey Spring Gap. The trail is an old roadbed which passes through a unique tunnel of mountain laurel. The last mile before Turkey Spring Gap is an excruciating climb that will humble even expert cyclists into dismounting. However, the upcoming descent and the outstanding views on Pilot Rock Trail make this short-lived agony worthwhile.

At Turkey Spring Gap, you can either backtrack on Laurel Mountain Trail for a fantastic descent or take the connector to Pilot Rock Trail for the scenic route. Pilot Rock Trail is steep in spots and has sharp switchbacks which should be negotiated with caution. There is a huge rock monolith at about 8 miles which is an ideal spot to rest and enjoy the spectacular views of Funneltop Mountain, the Pink Beds, and the South Mills River area. The loop ends with a 5-mile ride on F.R. 1206 back to your vehicle.

0.0 Begin at the Laurel Mountain trailhead. The trail begins a gradual ascent.

2.5 The trail passes through Rich Gap, a beautiful area with huge, old oaks and other hardwoods and an abundance of wildflowers in the spring.

3.4 A large boulder blocks the trail; the trail runs under a huge rock outcropping. During the winter months, there are frequently slender icicles hanging from this rock. This section of trail makes a great backdrop for photographs.

4.4 The trail passes through Johnson Gap.

5.3 The trail passes through Sassafras Gap.

5.7 The trail passes through Good Enough Gap and begins a tortuous ascent.

6.4 The trail reaches Turkey Spring Gap. Take a left on the connector to Pilot Rock Trail; it is marked with a yellow blaze. This is the last bit of climbing you will have to do. Hang in there—the work is almost over.

6.7 Turn left onto Pilot Rock Trail, which begins a rocky, steep descent.

7.5 This section of trail presents a number of switchbacks through groves of laurel, so watch your speed and ride cautiously.

8.1 There is a huge rock monolith which makes an ideal spot to pause and enjoy the breathtaking beauty of the area. Among the sights are views of the Pink Beds and Funneltop Mountain.

9.0 The trail ends on F.R. 1206. Turn left and proceed to the parking area at Yellow Gap. The road is mostly level, though there is a short climb at the end.

13.8 You will arrive back at your vehicle.

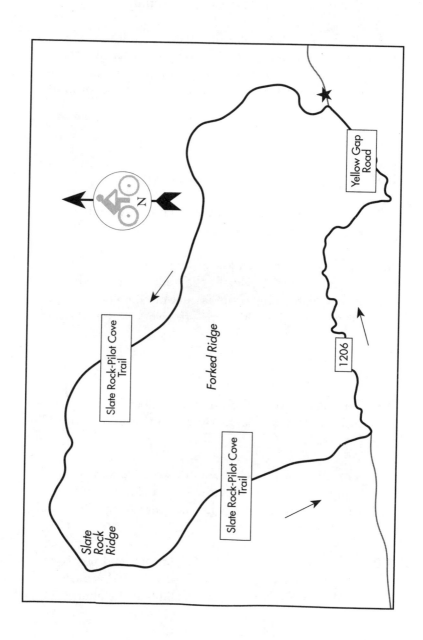

Slate Rock – Pilot Cove Trail Loop

Distance: 5.9 miles

Difficulty: Moderate

Riding surface: Single-track, unpaved forest-service road

Maps: 1. USGS 7.5 minute quadrangle,
      Dunsmore Mountain
   2. Pisgah District Trail Map

Access: From the ranger station, proceed north on U.S. 276 for 11 miles to the junction with F.R. 1206 (Yellow Gap Road). Turn right onto F.R. 1206 and drive approximately 7 miles to the parking area near the Slate Rock/ Pilot Cove trailhead.

Elevation change: The elevation at the parking area is about 2,800 feet. You will reach a maximum of about 3,800 feet at Slate Rock Ridge. From there, you will descend on Slate Rock/Pilot Cove Trail. The total elevation gain is 1,000 feet.

Season: This loop of trails is open year-round to mountain bikes.

Slate Rock / Pilot Cove Trail

This ride begins on a fairly steep ascending section of Slate Rock/Pilot Cove Trail. The trail moderates yet continues a gradual climb through a forest of birch, oak, and hemlock; a rich understory of laurel and rhododendron contributes to the lush, verdant beauty of this trail. A portion of Slate Rock/Pilot Cove Trail follows an old railroad bed. Near Slate Rock Ridge and the intersection with Slate Rock/Pilot Cove Trail, the trail narrows and squeezes through dense forest growth. To the left, you will see a small waterfall. After turning onto Slate Rock/Pilot Cove Trail, you will begin a moderate descent on a grassy, open trail punctuated with numerous creek crossings. At the end of the trail, turn left onto F.R. 1206 and cycle back to your vehicle.

0.0 From the parking area, begin the climb on Slate Rock/ Pilot Cove Trail.

2.4 A cascading waterfall is on the left; the trail is quite narrow at this point.

2.9 You will reach the intersection with Slate Rock/Pilot Cove Trail at Slate Rock Ridge. Turn to the left to begin the descent.

4.1 Slate Rock/Pilot Cove Trail ends at F.R. 1206. Turn left and cycle down to your parked car.

5.9 You will arrive back at the parking area.

Slate Rock / Pilot Cove Trail

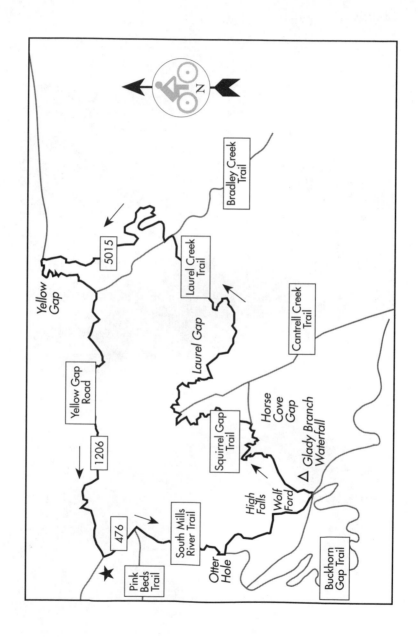

South Mills River Trail / Squirrel Gap Trail / Laurel Creek Trail / Bradley Creek Road / Yellow Gap Road Loop

Distance: 21.5 miles

Difficulty: Strenuous

Riding surface: Single-track, dirt road

Maps: 1. USGS 7.5 minute quadrangle, Dunsmore Mountain
2. USGS 7.5 minute quadrangle, Pisgah Forest
3. Pisgah District Trail Map

Access: From the ranger station, proceed north on U.S. 276 for 11 miles to the junction with F.R. 1206 (Yellow Gap Road). Turn right and proceed for about 3.5 miles to the parking pull-off on the left opposite F.R. 476 (Wolf Ford Road).

Elevation change: The ride begins at an elevation of 3,400 feet on F.R. 1206. It descends to 3,000 feet at Wolf Ford and gradually ascends to 3,400 feet at Horse Cove Gap and 3,480 feet at Laurel Gap. It then descends to 2,600 feet at Bradley Creek and climbs to 3,200 feet at Yellow Gap. The rolling grade of F.R. 1206 leads you on a descent to 2,800 feet and up again to 3,400 feet at the intersection with F.R. 476. The total elevation gain is 1,680 feet.

Season: This ride is open year-round to mountain bikes.

This long loop of trails and dirt roads is a favorite of serious cyclists. The ride begins on South Mills River Trail, which threads its way through dense, verdant creek-side flora, such as rhododendron, hemlock, and ferns; the sound of water spilling over river rocks fills the forest.

The surroundings change completely once you turn onto Squirrel Gap Trail, which weaves through hardwood coves as it passes into and out of numerous gaps, such as Squirrel Gap, Horse Cove Gap, and Laurel Gap. At 3,480 feet, Laurel Gap is the trail's highest point; during the winter season, it offers scenic views of Rich Mountain, Laurel Mountain, and the surrounding ridges and valleys.

Two small waterfalls are among the highlights of this loop: High Falls, on South Mills River Trail, and Glady Branch Waterfall, on Squirrel Gap Trail. Otter Hole, a popular swimming area in the South Mills River, can also be seen at the beginning of the loop.

Squirrel Gap Trail meanders around Laurel Mountain and Poundingstone Mountain before descending to the intersection with Laurel Creek Trail. A left turn onto this trail will lead you along the lush banks of Laurel Creek and onward to Bradley Creek Trail. After a short distance, you will turn right onto F.R. 5015 (Bradley Creek Road), a logging road which winds its way through sunny clearings as it ascends to Yellow Gap. During the summer, this climb is certain to leave you hot and parched. This ride is often referred to as "a four water-bottle ride," so be sure to bring plenty of water.

At Yellow Gap, turn left onto F.R. 1206 to cycle the last leg of the loop, which passes through Forked Ridge, Pilot Cove, and Grassy Lot Gap and across Dividing Ridge before intersecting with F.R. 476. F.R. 1206 is a beautiful, rolling dirt road bordered by mature hardwoods and some conifers. Lattice-like shadows decorate the road when the early-afternoon sun shines through the limbs of these trees.

0.0 From the parking pull-off on F.R. 1206, cycle down F.R. 476.

1.3 Cycle around the gate onto South Mills River Trail.

2.3 Pedal over the concrete bridge that spans South Mills River.

3.1 You will reach an intersection of trails; go straight.

4.0 Cross the creek, continue straight. Almost immediately, you will reach a T-intersection; bear left on the lower trail.

4.1 Cross a suspension bridge. Turn left onto the blue-blazed Squirrel Gap Trail; begin to climb.

4.7 The trail makes a hard left turn.

4.9 Glady Branch Waterfall is on the right.

5.1 A red-blazed trail is on the left; continue straight on Squirrel Gap Trail.

6.6 You will reach a high knoll. Bear left at the wooden sign to continue.

8.1 Cross Cantrell Creek. Cantrell Creek Trail intersects the trail; continue straight on Squirrel Gap Trail.

10.6 Poundingmill Trail intersects the trail; bear left to continue on Squirrel Gap Trail.

10.9 Turn left onto Laurel Creek Trail, which is marked with a yellow blaze.

11.5 You will reach a T-intersection; a creek is straight ahead. Turn right.

12.5 Cross Bradley Creek, a wide deep creek. Once you return to the trail, turn left onto Bradley Creek Trail.

12.7 Turn right onto a logging road, F.R. 5015.

16.6 Turn left onto Yellow Gap Road.

22.1 You will return to the intersection of F.R. 1206 (Yellow Gap Road) and F.R. 476, which marks the end of the ride.

Squirrel Gap Trail

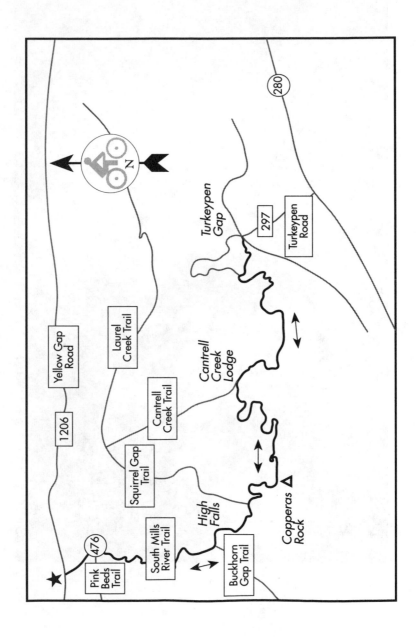

South Mills River Trail

Note: This ride is not a loop; it requires two vehicles. Set up a shuttle at the start on F.R. 1206 (Yellow Gap Road) and at the finish at Turkey Pen Gap.

Distance: 15 miles

Difficulty: Moderate

Riding surface: Single-track, short section of dirt road

Maps: 1. USGS 7.5 minute quadrangle, Pisgah Forest
2. USGS 7.5 minute quadrangle, Dunsmore Mountain
3. Pisgah District Trail Map

Access: From the ranger station, proceed north on U.S. 276 for 11 miles to the junction with F.R. 1206. Turn right and proceed about 3.5 miles to the parking pull-off on the left opposite F.R. 476 (Wolf Ford Road).

Elevation change: There is no remarkable elevation change on this ride. In fact, the ride begins at 3,200 feet on F.R. 1206 and ends at 2,400 feet at Turkey Pen Gap. The total elevation loss is 800 feet.

Season: This ride is open year-round to mountain bikes. However, since it requires you to ford the South Mills River a number of times, this loop should only be ridden during warm weather because of the risk of hypothermia. In addition, the river can be difficult, dangerous, or even impossible to ford after heavy rains. You would be well advised to avoid this trail under such circumstances.

Crossing the South Mills River

This is the ride for you if you hate to climb hills but don't mind getting wet. The trail meanders along the banks of the swiftly moving water of the South Mills River, crossing the river a total of 15 times. At 11 of these crossings, the river must be forded. (When fording the river, place your bike downstream; the current is stronger than it appears.) The remaining four crossings are over swinging bridges, which are welcome, dry alternatives. On the third crossing, be sure to notice Copperas Rock, a huge outcropping which seems to fill the river.

The trail weaves through fern-filled ravines and sun-dappled meadows but is mostly surrounded by heavy forest which allows no vistas of nearby mountain peaks. The banks of the river are lush with laurel, rhododendron, hemlock, and a stand of mixed hardwoods. The trail follows an old logging railroad for its entire distance and is therefore mostly level; a few of the old crossties can be seen in the trail. There are several portions of trail that are muddy and strewn with logs, a condition which requires you to carry your bike. This trail is most enjoyable during dry spells.

You will pass Cantrell Creek Trail, where the old Cantrell Creek Lodge once stood. Built in 1903 by Carl A. Schenck, the founder of the first school of forestry in America, it was moved from this site along the South Mills River to the Cradle of Forestry in 1978. All that remains here today is the lodge's chimney. A jocose hiker has placed a sign near the chimney reading, "Visitation only by ghosts."

0.0 From the parking pull-off on F.R. 1206, cycle down F.R. 476.

1.5 Cycle around the gate to begin South Mills River Trail.

3.2 There is an unmarked trail on the left that leads to High Falls.

3.8 This intersection of trails marks Wolf Ford. Cross the river and continue straight for the next 11 miles.

14.9 There is a fork in the trail; either fork will bring you to Turkey Pen Gap.

15.0 You will arrive at Turkey Pen Gap.

Boggy conditions exist in sections of South Mills River Trail.

Index